maps.com

WORLD HISTORY ATLAS

Contents

©2003 Maps.com, 6464 Hollister Avenue, Santa Barbara, CA 93117 / 800-929-4MAP / 805-685-3100. Third printing with revisions. Printed in Mexico.

Cover image: World map by Frederick deWit, 1660. Image from digital collection by Visual Language Library.

Visit the world's premier map website at http://www.maps.com for thousands of map resources, including driving directions, address finding, and downloadable maps. For additional educational map collections and resources, visit http://www.maps101.com.

EARLY CIVILIZATIONS, c. 8000–900 BCE

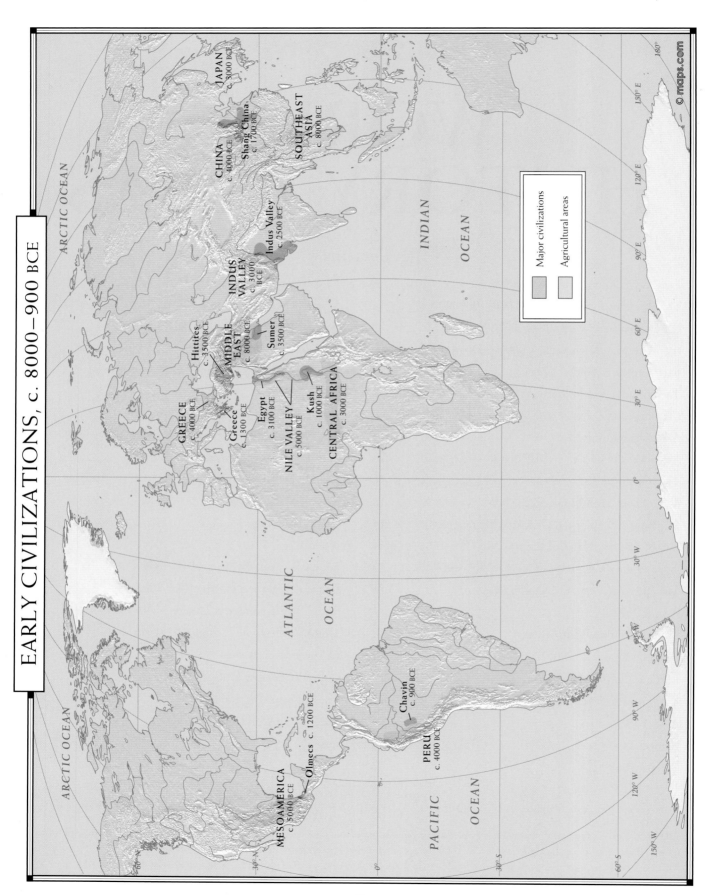

© maps.com

ARCTIC OCEAN

JAPAN
c. 3000 BCE

CHINA
c. 4000 BCE

Shang China
c. 1700 BCE

SOUTHEAST
ASIA
c. 8000 BCE

INDIAN
OCEAN

INDUS
VALLEY
c. 3000
BCE

Indus Valley
c. 2500 BCE

Hittites
c. 3500 BCE

MIDDLE
EAST
c. 8000 BCE

Sumer
c. 3500 BCE

GREECE
c. 4000 BCE

Greece
c. 1300 BCE

Egypt
c. 3100 BCE

Kush
c. 1000 BCE

CENTRAL AFRICA
c. 3000 BCE

NILE VALLEY
c. 5000 BCE

ARCTIC OCEAN

ATLANTIC

OCEAN

MESOAMERICA
c. 5000 BCE

Olmecs c. 1200 BCE

Chavin
c. 900 BCE

PERU
c. 4000 BCE

PACIFIC

OCEAN

| | Major civilizations |
| | Agricultural areas |

160°

150° E

120° E

90° E

60° E

30° E

0°

30° W

90° W

120° W

150° W

– 2 –

THE SPREAD OF AGRICULTURE, c. 10,000–1000 BCE

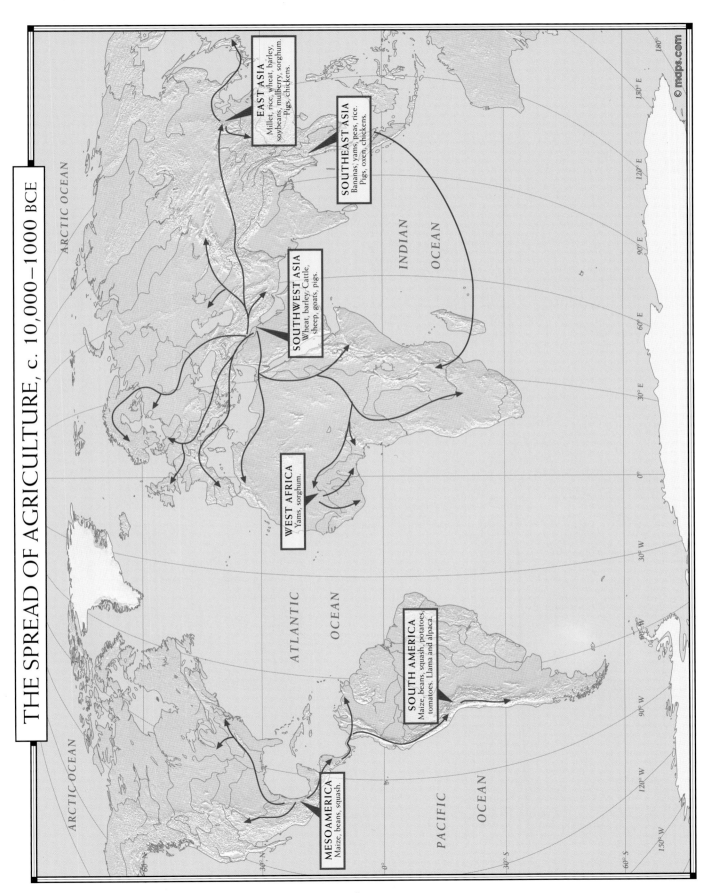

EAST ASIA
Millet, rice, wheat, barley, soybeans, mulberry, sorghum. Pigs, chickens.

SOUTHEAST ASIA
Bananas, yams, peas, rice. Pigs, oxen, chickens.

SOUTHWEST ASIA
Wheat, barley, Cattle, sheep, goats, pigs.

WEST AFRICA
Yams, sorghum.

SOUTH AMERICA
Maize, beans, squash, potatoes, tomatoes. Llama and alpaca.

MESOAMERICA
Maize, beans, squash.

ARCTIC OCEAN

INDIAN OCEAN

ATLANTIC OCEAN

PACIFIC OCEAN

ARCTIC OCEAN

© maps.com

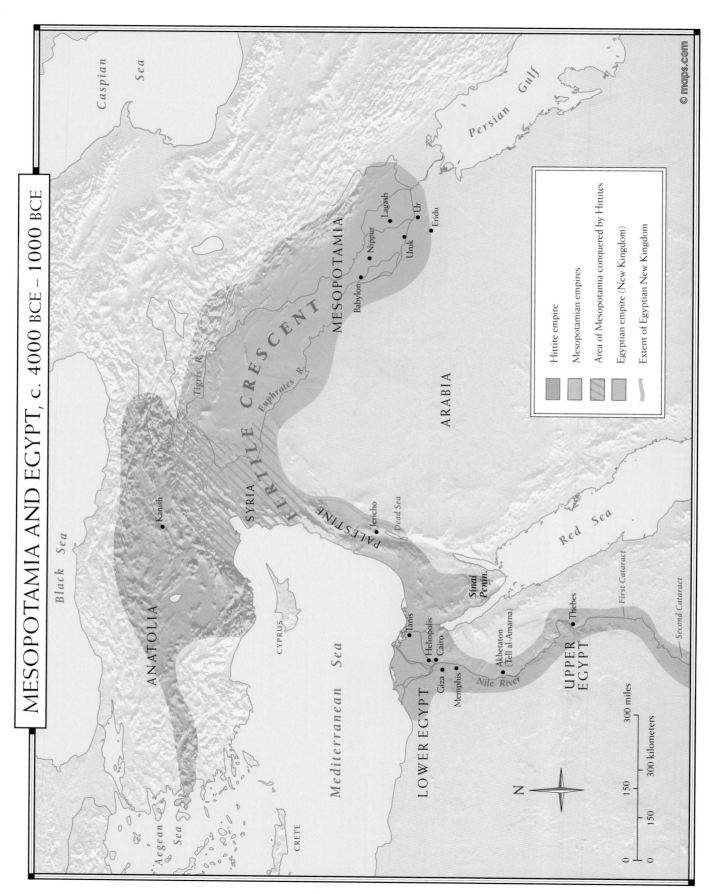

MESOPOTAMIA AND EGYPT, c. 4000 BCE – 1000 BCE

Caspian Sea

Persian Gulf

© maps.com

MESOPOTAMIA

Lagash
Ur
Eridu
Nippur
Uruk
Babylon

Legend
- Hittite empire
- Mesopotamian empires
- Area of Mesopotamia conquered by Hittites
- Egyptian empire (New Kingdom)
- Extent of Egyptian New Kingdom

FERTILE CRESCENT

SYRIA

Tigris R.

Euphrates R.

Kanish

Black Sea

ANATOLIA

PALESTINE

Jericho

Dead Sea

ARABIA

CYPRUS

Mediterranean Sea

Red Sea

Sinai Penin.

Tanis
Heliopolis
Cairo
Giza
Memphis
Akhetaton
(Tell al-Amarna)

Nile River

Thebes

First Cataract

Second Cataract

UPPER EGYPT

LOWER EGYPT

Aegean Sea

CRETE

300 miles

300 kilometers

0   150   300

0   150   300

N

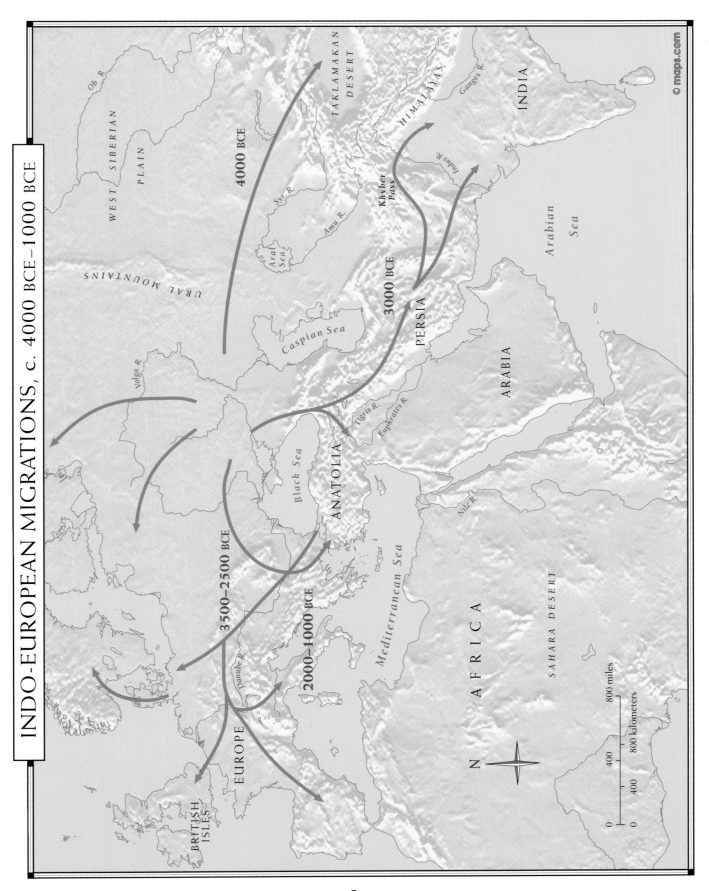

INDO-EUROPEAN MIGRATIONS, c. 4000 BCE–1000 BCE

4000 BCE

3000 BCE

3500–2500 BCE

2000–1000 BCE

WEST SIBERIAN PLAIN

Ob R.

TAKLAMAKAN DESERT

HIMALAYAS

Ganges R.

INDIA

Syr R.

Amu R.

Aral Sea

URAL MOUNTAINS

Khyber Pass

Indus R.

Arabian Sea

Caspian Sea

PERSIA

Volga R.

Tigris R.

Euphrates R.

ARABIA

Black Sea

ANATOLIA

Nile R.

Mediterranean Sea

AFRICA

SAHARA DESERT

Danube R.

EUROPE

BRITISH ISLES

N

800 miles

800 kilometers

0   400   800

0   400   800

© maps.com

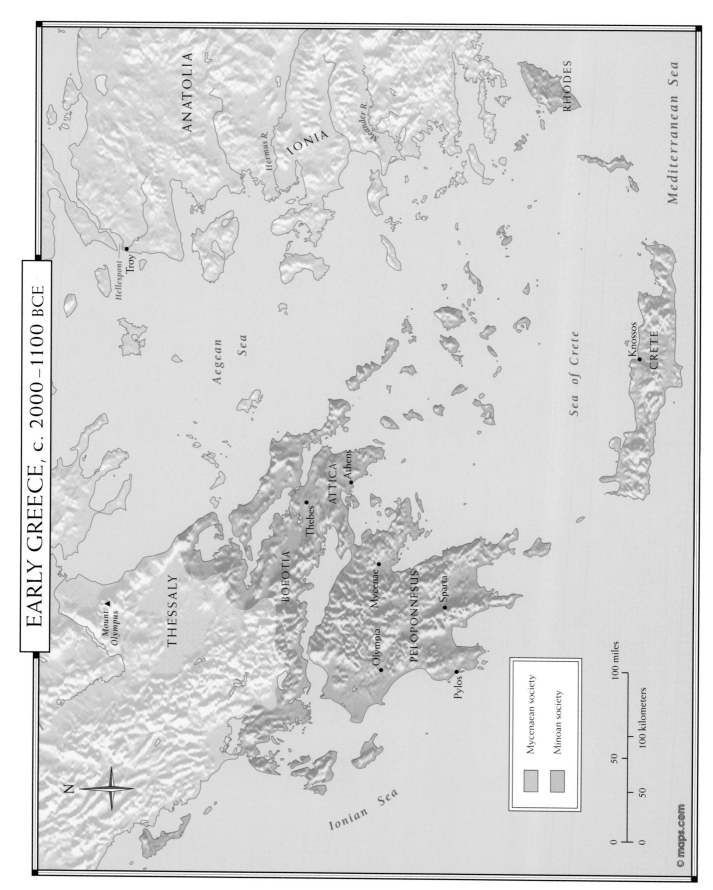

EARLY GREECE, c. 2000 – 1100 BCE

ANATOLIA

IONIA

Hermus R.

Meander R.

RHODES

Mediterranean Sea

Hellespont

Troy

Aegean Sea

Sea of Crete

Knossos

CRETE

Mount Olympus

THESSALY

BOEOTIA

Thebes

ATTICA

Athens

Mycenae

Olympia

PELOPONNESUS

Sparta

Pylos

Ionian Sea

N

Mycenaean society

Minoan society

100 miles

100 kilometers

50

50

0

0

© maps.com

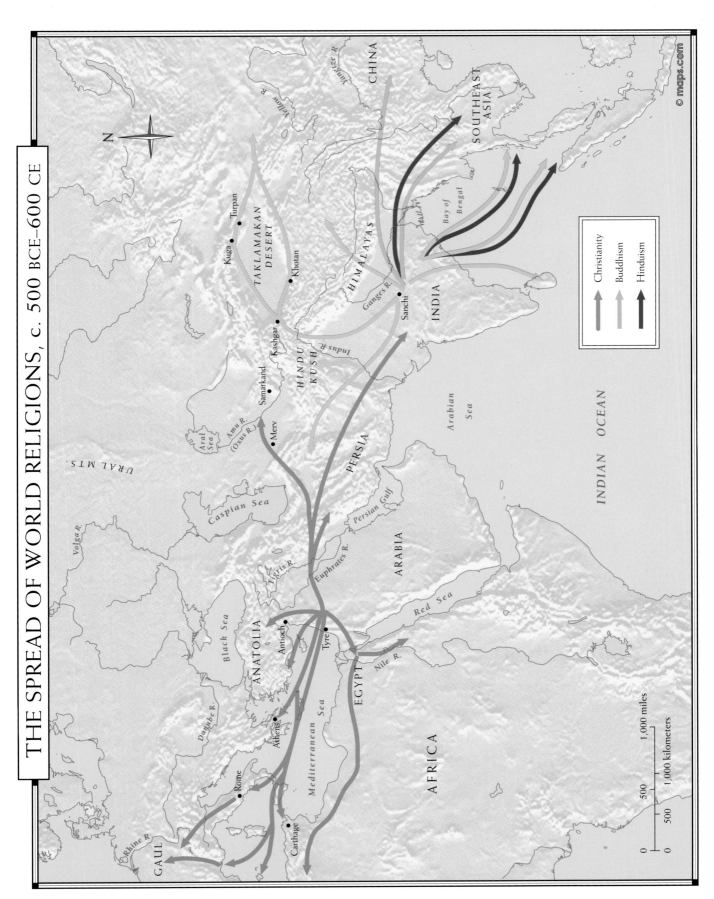

THE SPREAD OF WORLD RELIGIONS, c. 500 BCE–600 CE

Legend:
- Christianity
- Buddhism
- Hinduism

CHINA

SOUTHEAST ASIA

Yangtze R.

Yellow R.

Turpan

Kuga

TAKLAMAKAN DESERT

Khotan

Kashgar

HINDU KUSH

HIMALAYAS

Ganges R.

Sanchi

Indus R.

INDIA

Bay of Bengal

Samarkand

Amu R. (Oxus R.)

Merv

Aral Sea

URAL MTS.

Volga R.

Caspian Sea

PERSIA

Arabian Sea

INDIAN OCEAN

Persian Gulf

Tigris R.

Euphrates R.

ARABIA

Red Sea

Black Sea

ANATOLIA

Antioch

Tyre

EGYPT

Nile R.

Danube R.

Athens

Mediterranean Sea

Rome

Carthage

GAUL

Rhine R.

AFRICA

N

1,000 miles

1,000 kilometers

500

500

0

0

© maps.com

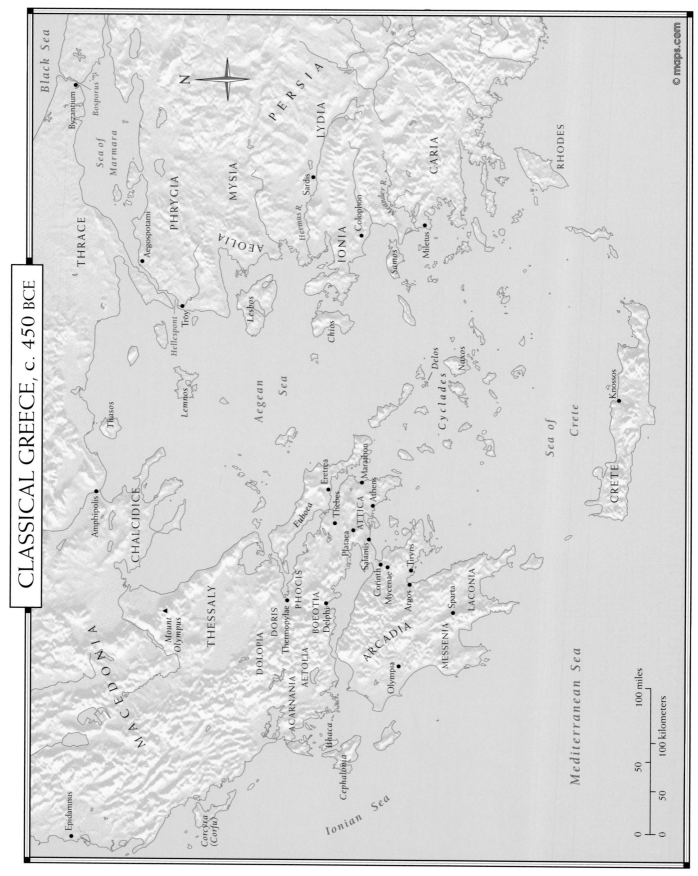

CLASSICAL GREECE, c. 450 BCE

Black Sea

Byzantium

Bosporus

Sea of Marmara

THRACE

PERSIA

LYDIA

MYSIA

PHRYGIA

Aegospotami

AEOLIA

Sardis

Hermus R.

Colophon

Maeander R.

CARIA

RHODES

IONIA

Samos

Miletus

Troy

Hellespont

Lesbos

Chios

Thasos

Lemnos

Aegean Sea

Cyclades

Delos

Naxos

Sea of Crete

Crete

Knossos

CRETE

Amphipolis

CHALCIDICE

Euboea

Eretria

Marathon

Thebes

Athens

ATTICA

Plataea

Salamis

Corinth

Tiryns

Mycenae

Argos

Sparta

LACONIA

MESSENIA

Olympia

ARCADIA

Mount Olympus

THESSALY

DOLOPIA

DORIS

PHOCIS

Thermopylae

BOEOTIA

Delphi

AETOLIA

ACARNANIA

Ithaca

Cephalonia

Corcyra (Corfu)

Ionian Sea

Epidamnus

MACEDONIA

Mediterranean Sea

100 miles

100 kilometers

50

50

0

0

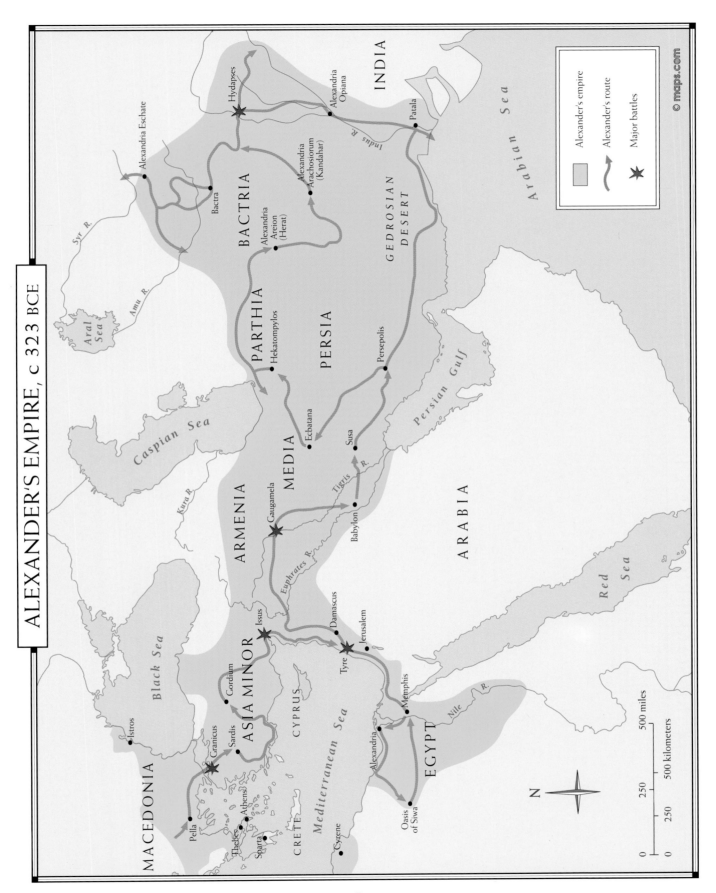

ALEXANDER'S EMPIRE, c 323 BCE

Alexander's empire
Alexander's route
Major battles

© maps.com

INDIA

Arabian Sea

Hydapses
Alexandria Opiana
Patala
Indus R.
BACTRIA
Alexandria Eschate
Bactra
Alexandria Arachosiorum (Kandahar)
Alexandria Areion (Herat)
GEDROSIAN DESERT
Syr R.
Amu R.
PARTHIA
PERSIA
Aral Sea
Hekatompylos
Persepolis
MEDIA
Caspian Sea
Echatana
Susa
Persian Gulf
ARMENIA
Tigris R.
Gaugamela
Kura R.
Babylon
Euphrates R.
ARABIA
Damascus
Jerusalem
Issus
Red Sea
ASIA MINOR
Gordium
Tyre
Sardis
Granicus
Memphis
CYPRUS
Black Sea
Istros
Mediterranean Sea
Alexandria
Nile R.
Pella
MACEDONIA
Athens
Thebes
Sparta
EGYPT
CRETE
Cyrene
Oasis of Siwa

N

500 miles
500 kilometers
250
250
0
0

– 9 –

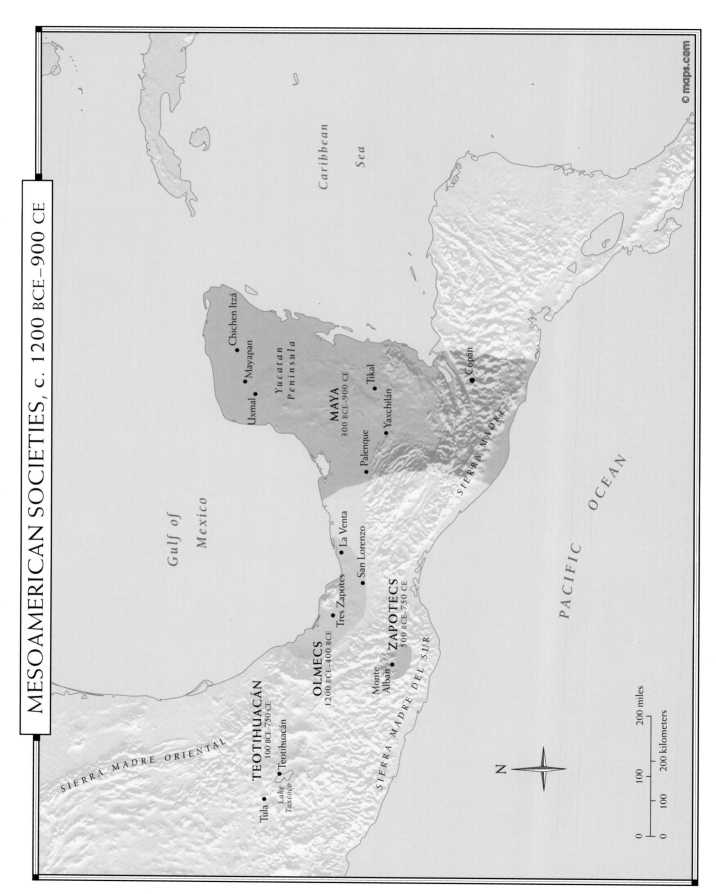

MESOAMERICAN SOCIETIES, c. 1200 BCE–900 CE

Caribbean Sea

Chichen Itzá

Mayapan
Uxmal

Yucatan Peninsula

MAYA
300 BCE–900 CE

Tikal

Yaxchilán

Palenque

Copán

SIERRA MADRE

Gulf of Mexico

La Venta

San Lorenzo

Tres Zapotes

OLMECS
1200 BCE–400 BCE

ZAPOTECS
500 BCE–750 CE

Monte Albán

SIERRA MADRE DEL SUR

TEOTIHUACÁN
100 BCE–750 CE

Teotihuacán

Tula

Lake Texcoco

SIERRA MADRE ORIENTAL

PACIFIC OCEAN

N

| 0 | 100 | 200 miles |
| 0 | 100 | 200 kilometers |

© maps.com

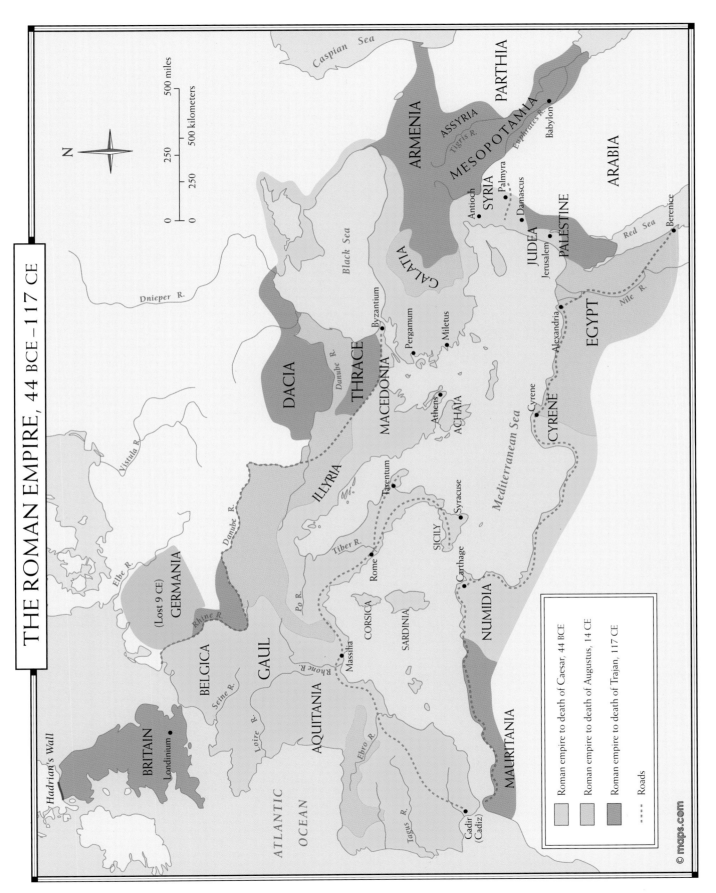

THE ROMAN EMPIRE, 44 BCE – 117 CE

N

500 miles

500 kilometers

250

250

250

0

0

Caspian Sea

PARTHIA

ARMENIA

ASSYRIA

MESOPOTAMIA

Tigris R.

Euphrates R.

Babylon

ARABIA

Antioch

SYRIA

Palmyra

Damascus

PALESTINE

JUDEA

Jerusalem

Red Sea

Berenice

Black Sea

GALATIA

Dnieper R.

Byzantium

Pergamum

Miletus

Nile R.

Alexandria

EGYPT

THRACE

DACIA

MACEDONIA

Danube R.

Athens

ACHAIA

Cyrene

CYRENE

Mediterranean Sea

Vistula R.

ILLYRIA

Tarentum

Danube R.

SICILY

Syracuse

Elbe R.

GERMANIA

(Lost 9 CE)

Rhine R.

Po R.

Tiber R.

Rome

CORSICA

SARDINIA

Carthage

NUMIDIA

BELGICA

GAUL

Seine R.

Massilia

Rhone R.

MAURITANIA

AQUITANIA

Loire R.

Hadrian's Wall

BRITAIN

Londinium

Ebro R.

ATLANTIC
OCEAN

Tagus R.

Cadir
(Cadiz)

Roman empire to death of Caesar, 44 BCE

Roman empire to death of Augustus, 14 CE

Roman empire to death of Trajan, 117 CE

Roads

© maps.com

– 11 –

MAJOR STATES AND CULTURES OF THE WORLD, c. 100 CE

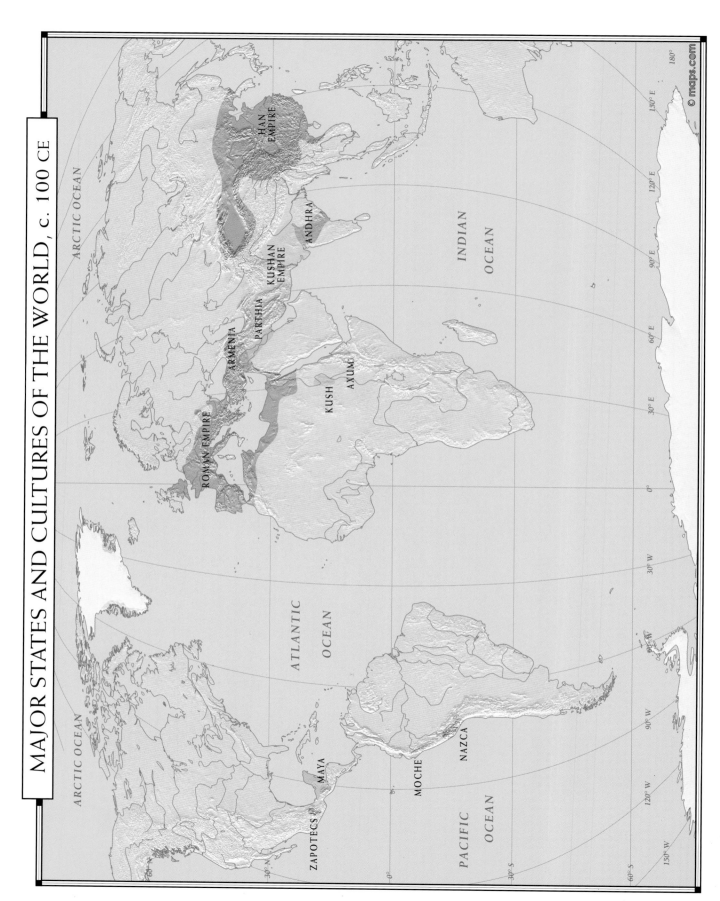

ARCTIC OCEAN

HAN EMPIRE

ANDHRA

KUSHAN EMPIRE

PARTHIA

ARMENIA

INDIAN OCEAN

KUSH

AXUM

ROMAN EMPIRE

ATLANTIC OCEAN

ARCTIC OCEAN

ZAPOTECS

MAYA

MOCHE

NAZCA

PACIFIC OCEAN

© maps.com

180°
150° E
120° E
90° E
60° E
30° E
0°
30° W
90° W
120° W
150° W

60° N
30° N
0°
30° S
60° S

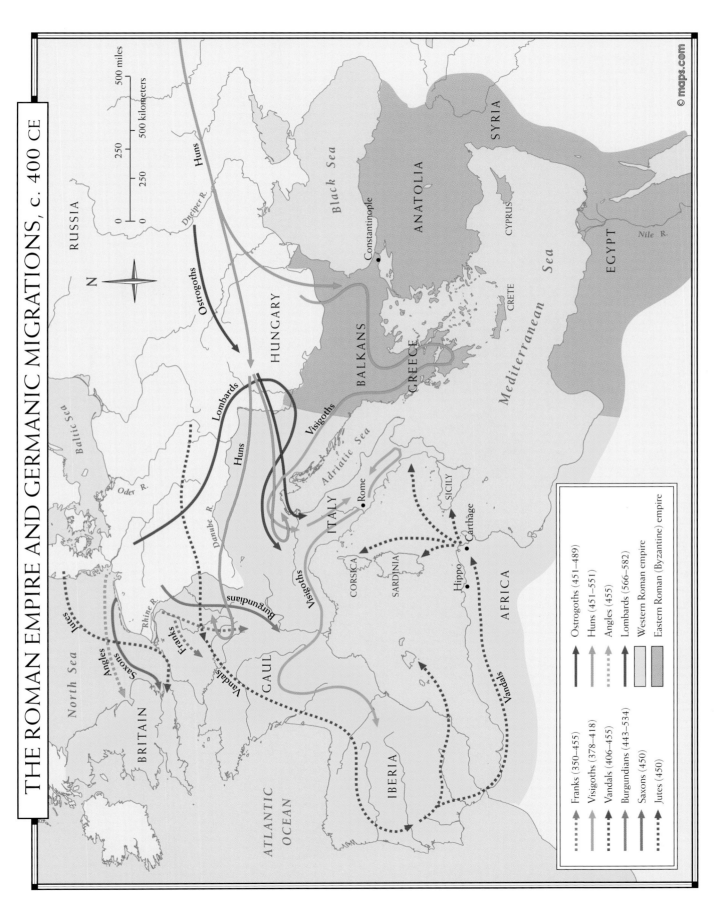

THE ROMAN EMPIRE AND GERMANIC MIGRATIONS, c. 400 CE

RUSSIA

Black Sea

ANATOLIA

SYRIA

CYPRUS

Constantinople

CRETE

GREECE

EGYPT

Nile R.

Mediterranean Sea

BALKANS

Adriatic Sea

Huns

Dnieper R.

Ostrogoths

HUNGARY

Lombards

Visigoths

Baltic Sea

Oder R.

Danube R.

Huns

Rhine R.

Burgundians

Visigoths

ITALY

Rome

CORSICA

SARDINIA

SICILY

Carthage

Hippo

AFRICA

GAUL

Franks

Vandals

Burgundians

BRITAIN

Angles

Saxons

Jutes

IBERIA

Vandals

North Sea

ATLANTIC OCEAN

N

500 miles

500 kilometers

250

250

250

0

0

© maps.com

Franks (350–455)	Ostrogoths (451–489)
Visigoths (378–418)	Huns (451–551)
Vandals (406–455)	Angles (455)
Burgundians (443–534)	Lombards (566–582)
Saxons (450)	Western Roman empire
Jutes (450)	Eastern Roman (Byzantine) empire

EUROPE AND THE BYZANTINE EMPIRE, 525–565 CE

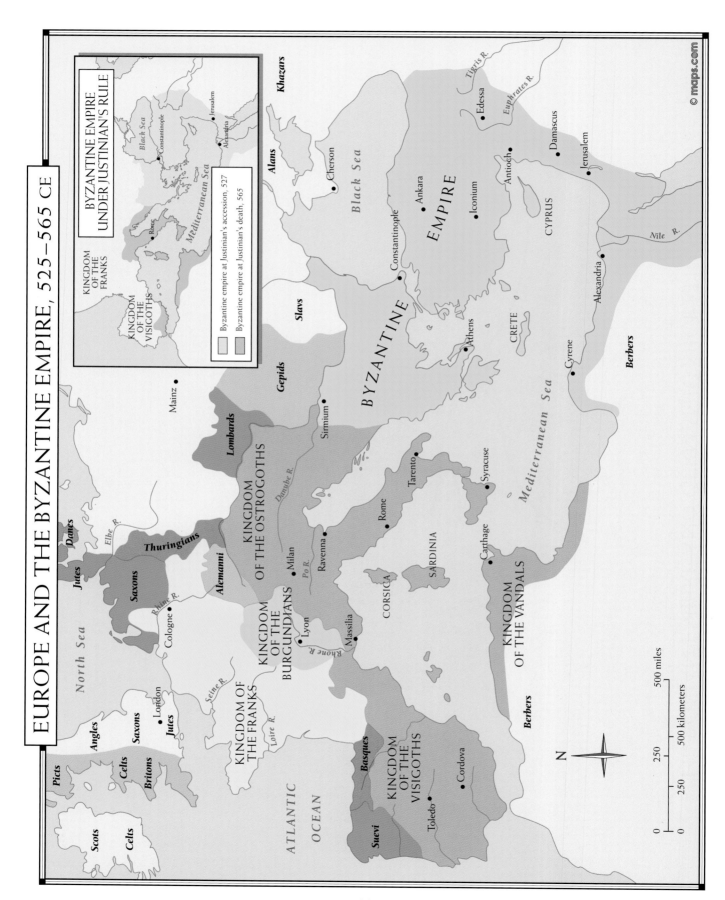

BYZANTINE EMPIRE UNDER JUSTINIAN'S RULE

KINGDOM OF THE FRANKS

KINGDOM OF THE VISIGOTHS

Mediterranean Sea

Rome

Constantinople

Black Sea

Alexandria

Jerusalem

Byzantine empire at Justinian's accession, 527

Byzantine empire at Justinian's death, 565

Khazars

Alans

Cherson

Black Sea

Tigris R.

Euphrates R.

Edessa

Damascus

Ankara

Iconium

Antioch

Jerusalem

BYZANTINE EMPIRE

Constantinople

CYPRUS

Nile R.

Athens

Alexandria

CRETE

Cyrene

Berbers

Slavs

Gepids

Sirmium

Mainz

Lombards

KINGDOM OF THE OSTROGOTHS

Danube R.

Mediterranean Sea

Syracuse

Tarento

Rome

Milan

Po R.

Ravenna

SARDINIA

Carthage

KINGDOM OF THE VANDALS

Berbers

Danes

Elbe R.

Thuringians

Jutes

Saxons

Alemanni

Cologne

Rhine R.

KINGDOM OF THE BURGUNDIANS

Lyon

Massilia

Rhône R.

CORSICA

North Sea

Angles

Saxons

Jutes

London

Seine R.

KINGDOM OF THE FRANKS

Loire R.

Picts

Celts

Britons

Scots

Celts

ATLANTIC OCEAN

Basques

KINGDOM OF THE VISIGOTHS

Cordova

Toledo

Suevi

N

0   250   500 miles

0   250   500 kilometers

© maps.com

— 14 —

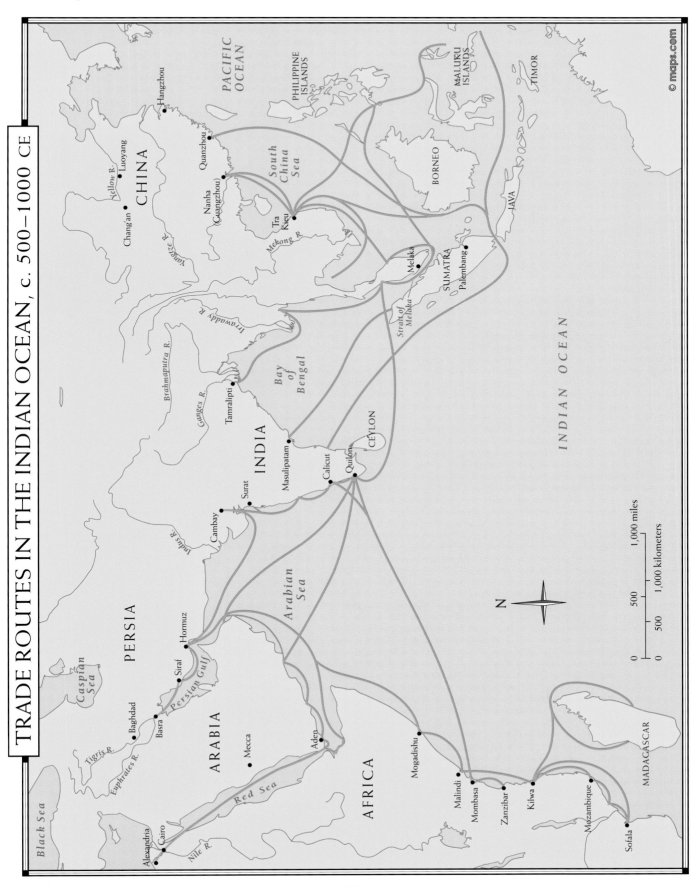

TRADE ROUTES IN THE INDIAN OCEAN, c. 500–1000 CE

PACIFIC OCEAN

PHILIPPINE ISLANDS

MALUKU ISLANDS

TIMOR

Hangzhou

Luoyang

Yellow R.

CHINA

Quanzhou

Nanha (Guangzhou)

Guangzhou

Chang'an

Yangtze R.

South China Sea

BORNEO

JAVA

Tra Kieu

Mekong R.

SUMATRA

Melaka

Palembang

Strait of Melaka

Brahmaputra R.

Irrawaddy R.

Ganges R.

Bay of Bengal

INDIAN OCEAN

Tamralipti

INDIA

Masulipatam

CEYLON

Calicut

Quilon

Surat

Cambay

Indus R.

Arabian Sea

PERSIA

Caspian Sea

Hormuz

Siraf

Persian Gulf

Baghdad

Basra

Tigris R.

ARABIA

Mecca

Euphrates R.

Aden

Red Sea

AFRICA

Mogadishu

Malindi

Mombasa

Zanzibar

Kilwa

Mozambique

Sofala

MADAGASCAR

Black Sea

Alexandria

Cairo

Nile R.

N

1,000 miles

1,000 kilometers

500

500

0

0

© maps.com

THE SPREAD OF ISLAM, 622 – 750 CE

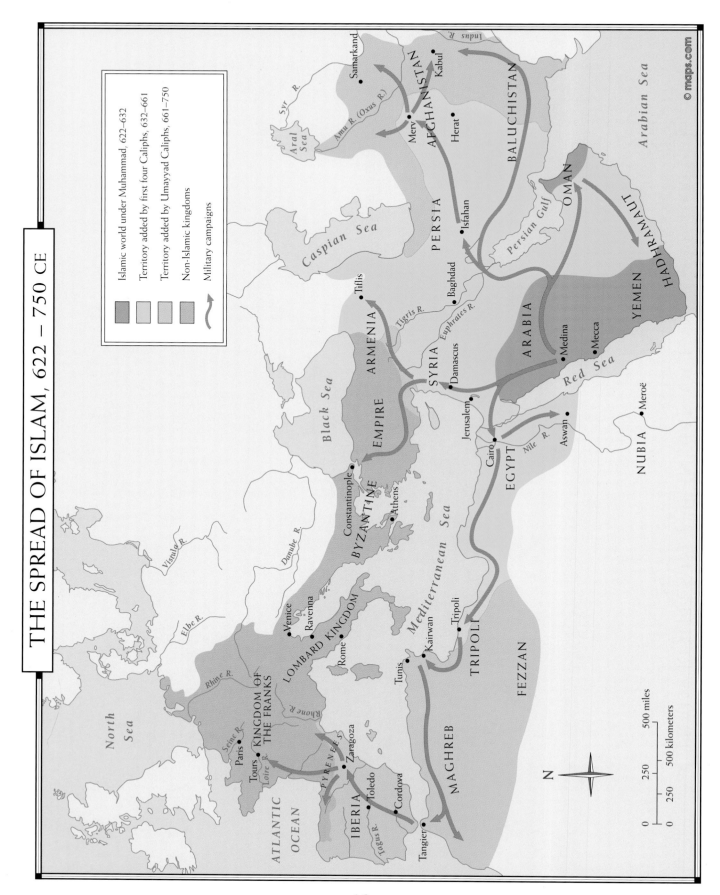

Legend:
- Islamic world under Muhammad, 622–632
- Territory added by first four Caliphs, 632–661
- Territory added by Umayyad Caliphs, 661–750
- Non-Islamic kingdoms
- Military campaigns

© maps.com

Seas and Oceans: Arabian Sea, Caspian Sea, Black Sea, Mediterranean Sea, Red Sea, Persian Gulf, North Sea, Atlantic Ocean, Aral Sea

Rivers: Syr R., Amu R. (Oxus R.), Indus R., Tigris R., Euphrates R., Nile R., Danube R., Vistula R., Elbe R., Rhine R., Rhône R., Loire R., Seine R., Tagus R.

Regions: AFGHANISTAN, BALUCHISTAN, PERSIA, OMAN, HADHRAMAUT, YEMEN, ARABIA, SYRIA, ARMENIA, BYZANTINE EMPIRE, EGYPT, NUBIA, TRIPOLI, FEZZAN, MAGHREB, IBERIA, KINGDOM OF THE FRANKS, LOMBARD KINGDOM, PYRENEES

Cities: Samarkand, Kabul, Merv, Herat, Isfahan, Baghdad, Tiflis, Damascus, Jerusalem, Medina, Mecca, Meroë, Aswan, Cairo, Constantinople, Athens, Venice, Ravenna, Rome, Tripoli, Kairwan, Tunis, Tangier, Cordova, Toledo, Zaragoza, Tours, Paris

N

0   250   500 miles
0   250   500 kilometers

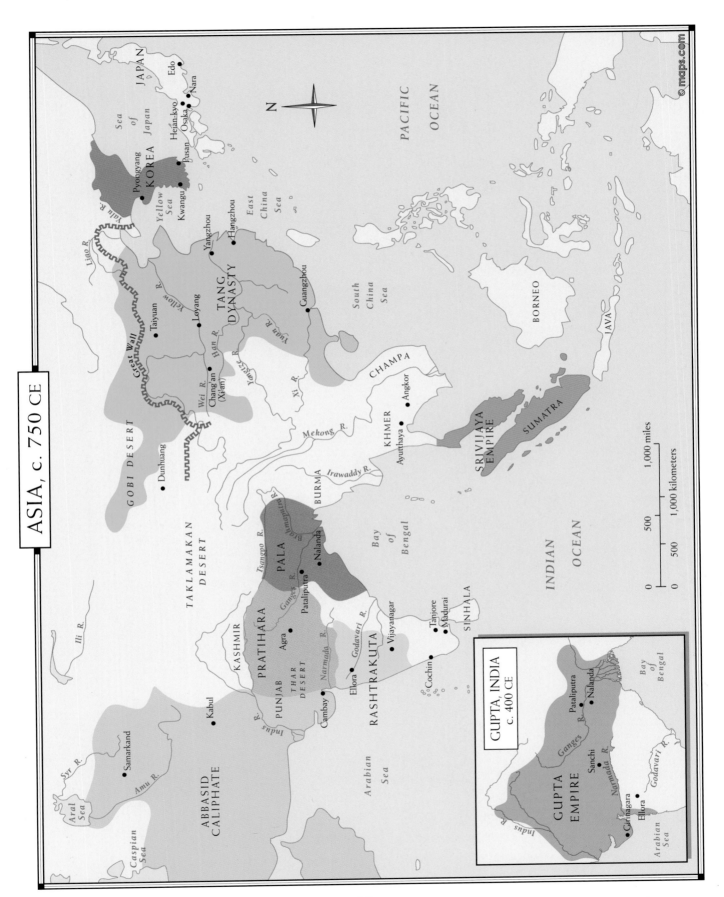

ASIA, c. 750 CE

JAPAN
Edo
Nara
Heian-kyo
Osaka
Sea of Japan
KOREA
Pyongyang
Kwangu
Busan
Yellow Sea

PACIFIC OCEAN

Yangzhou
Hangzhou
East China Sea

TANG DYNASTY
Taiyuan
Loyang
Chang'an (Xi'an)
Yellow R.
Han R.
Wei R.
Yangzi R.
Yuan R.
Guangzhou
Xi R.

South China Sea

Great Wall
GOBI DESERT
Liao R.
Yalu R.
Dunhuang

TAKLAMAKAN DESERT

BURMA
Irawaddy R.
Mekong R.

CHAMPA
Angkor
KHMER
Ayuthaya

SRIVIJAYA EMPIRE
SUMATRA
BORNEO
JAVA

Tsangpo R.
Brahmaputra R.
PALA
Nalanda
Pataliputra
Ganges R.
PRATIHARA
Agra
KASHMIR
PUNJAB
THAR DESERT
Narmada R.
Indus R.
Kabul
Cambay
Ellora
Godavari R.
RASHTRAKUTA
Vijayanagar
Cochin
Tanjore
Madurai
SINHALA

Bay of Bengal

INDIAN OCEAN

Arabian Sea

ABBASID CALIPHATE
Samarkand
Syr R.
Amu R.
Aral Sea
Caspian Sea
Ili R.

1,000 miles
500
0
1,000 kilometers
500
0

GUPTA, INDIA c. 400 CE

Pataliputra
Nalanda
Ganges R.
Sanchi
Narmada R.
Godavari R.
GUPTA EMPIRE
Girnagara
Ellora
Indus R.
Arabian Sea
Bay of Bengal

© maps.com

— 17 —

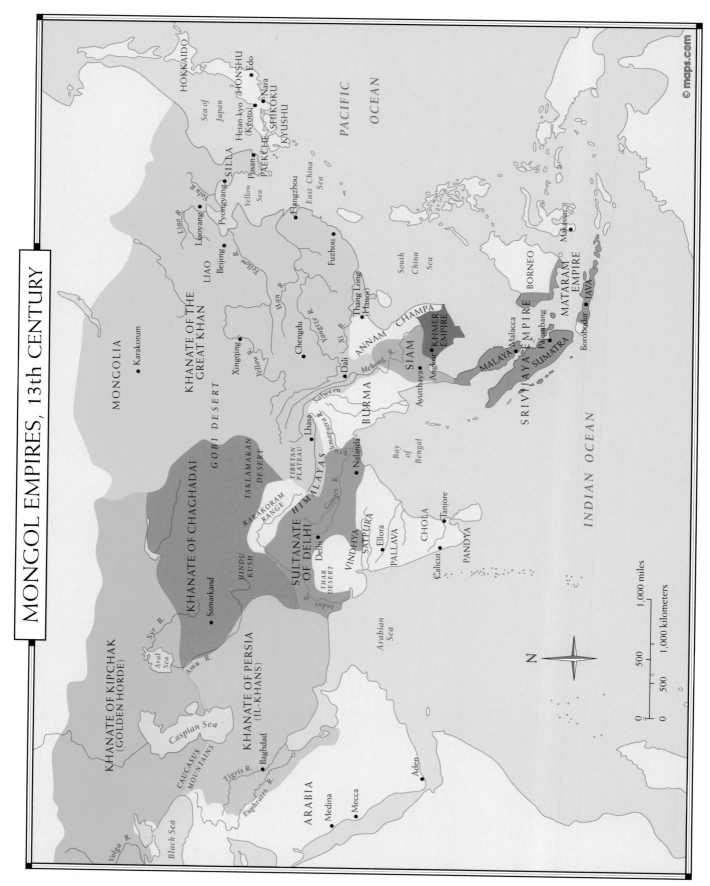

MONGOL EMPIRES, 13th CENTURY

HOKKAIDO

Sea of Japan

HONSHU
Edo
Heian-kyo (Kyoto)
Nara
SHIKOKU
KYUSHU

SILLA
Pyongyang
Pusan
PAEKCHE

Yellow Sea

Liao R.
Liaoyang
Beijing
LIAO

Itil R.

PACIFIC

OCEAN

Hangzhou

East China Sea

Fuzhou

MONGOLIA

Karakorum

KHANATE OF THE GREAT KHAN

GOBI DESERT

South China Sea

Yellow R.
Xingqing
Han R.
Yellow R.
Chengdu
Yangtze R.
Dali
Xi R.
Mekong R.

Thang Long (Hanoi)
ANNAM
CHAMPA

SIAM
Angkor
KHMER EMPIRE
Ayutthaya

BORNEO

MATARAM EMPIRE
Makassar

SRIVIJAYA EMPIRE
Malacca
MALAYA
Palembang
SUMATRA
Borobudur
JAVA

TAKLAMAKAN DESERT

KHANATE OF CHAGHADAI

KARAKORAM RANGE

TIBETAN PLATEAU
Lhasa
HIMALAYAS
Salween R.
Brahmaputra R.
BURMA

Nalanda
Ganges R.

Bay of Bengal

INDIAN OCEAN

Samarkand

HINDU KUSH

SULTANATE OF DELHI
Delhi
VINDHYA
SATPURA
Ellora
PALLAVA

THAR DESERT

Indus R.

CHOLA
Tanjore

Calicut
PANDYA

KHANATE OF KIPCHAK (GOLDEN HORDE)

Syr R.
Aral Sea
Amu R.

KHANATE OF PERSIA (IL-KHANS)

Caspian Sea

CAUCASUS MOUNTAINS
Tigris R.
Baghdad

Arabian Sea

Black Sea

Euphrates R.

ARABIA
Medina
Mecca

Aden

N

1,000 miles
1,000 kilometers
500
500
0
0

© maps.com

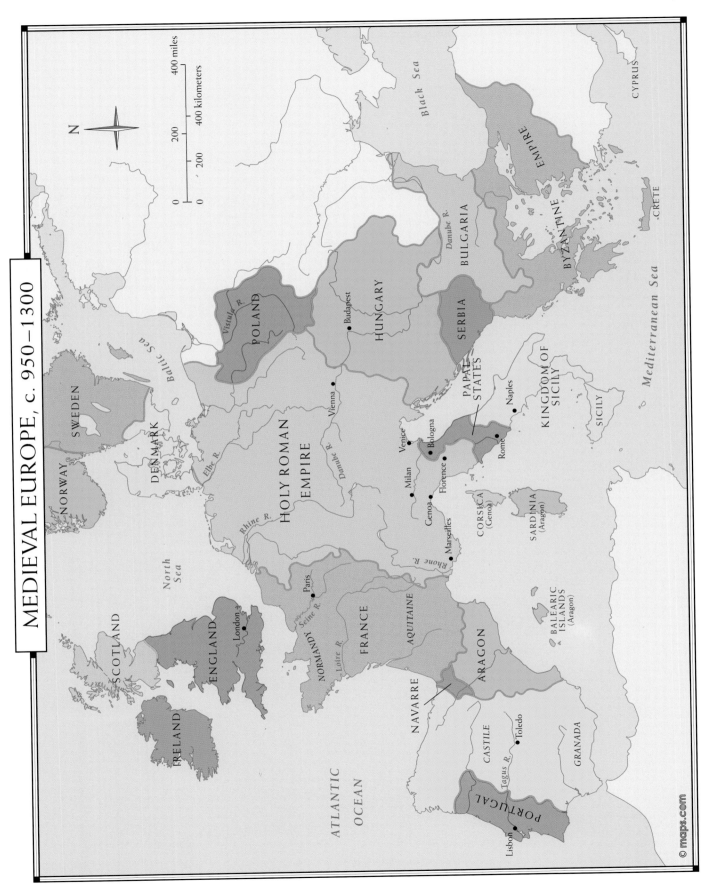

MEDIEVAL EUROPE, c. 950–1300

N

400 miles
400 kilometers
200
200
0
0

ATLANTIC OCEAN

North Sea

Baltic Sea

Black Sea

Mediterranean Sea

NORWAY

SWEDEN

DENMARK

SCOTLAND

IRELAND

ENGLAND
London

Elbe R.

POLAND

Vistula R.

HOLY ROMAN EMPIRE

HUNGARY

Budapest

Vienna

Danube R.

Danube R.

BULGARIA

SERBIA

BYZANTINE EMPIRE

CYPRUS

CRETE

NORMANDY

Paris

Seine R.

Loire R.

FRANCE

Rhine R.

AQUITAINE

Rhône R.

Marseilles

Milan

Genoa

Venice

Bologna

Florence

PAPAL STATES

Rome

Naples

KINGDOM OF SICILY

SICILY

CORSICA (Genoa)

SARDINIA (Aragon)

BALEARIC ISLANDS (Aragon)

NAVARRE

ARAGON

CASTILE

Toledo

Tagus R.

GRANADA

PORTUGAL

Lisbon

© maps.com

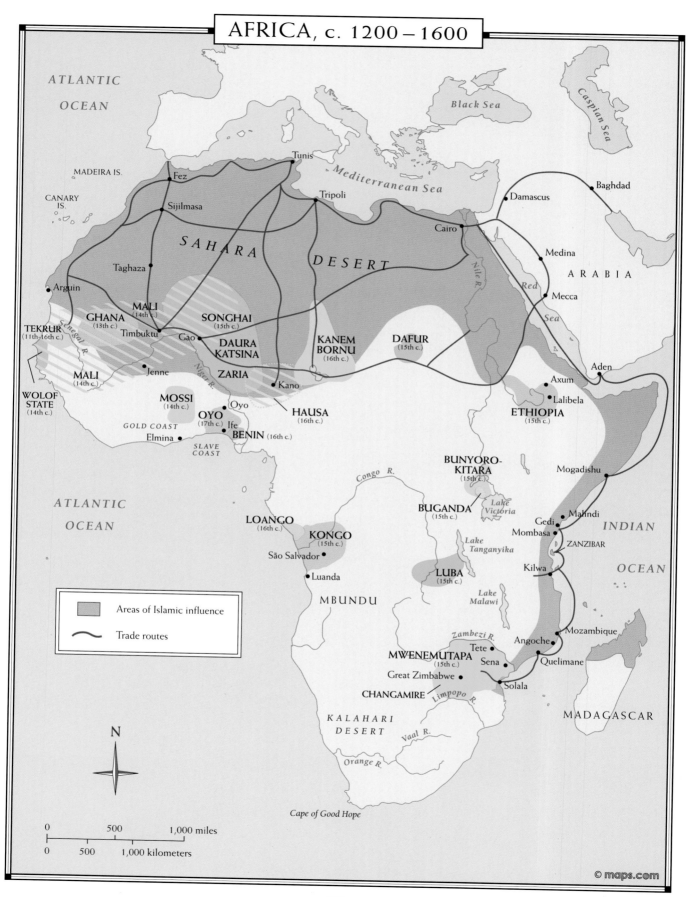

AFRICA, c. 1200 – 1600

ATLANTIC OCEAN

Black Sea

Caspian Sea

MADEIRA IS.

CANARY IS.

Fez

Tunis

Mediterranean Sea

Tripoli

Damascus

Baghdad

Sijilmasa

Cairo

S A H A R A   D E S E R T

Medina

A R A B I A

Taghaza

Mecca

Red Sea

Nile R.

Arguin

MALI (14th c.)

GHANA (13th c.)

SONGHAI (15th c.)

Timbuktu

Gao

DAURA KATSINA

KANEM BORNU (16th c.)

DAFUR (15th c.)

Aden

Axum

TEKRUR (11th-16th c.)

Senegal R.

ZARIA

Lalibela

Jenne

Niger R.

Kano

ETHIOPIA (15th c.)

MALI (14th c.)

WOLOF STATE (14th c.)

MOSSI (14th c.)

Oyo

HAUSA (16th c.)

OYO (17th c.)

Ife

GOLD COAST

Elmina

BENIN (16th c.)

SLAVE COAST

Mogadishu

BUNYORO-KITARA (15th c.)

Congo R.

BUGANDA (15th c.)

Lake Victoria

Malindi

Gedi

INDIAN

ATLANTIC OCEAN

LOANGO (16th c.)

KONGO (15th c.)

São Salvador

Lake Tanganyika

Mombasa

ZANZIBAR

Kilwa

OCEAN

Luanda

LUBA (15th c.)

MBUNDU

Lake Malawi

Mozambique

Zambezi R.

Tete

Angoche

MWENEMUTAPA (15th c.)

Sena

Quelimane

Great Zimbabwe

Solala

CHANGAMIRE

Limpopo R.

MADAGASCAR

KALAHARI DESERT

Vaal R.

Orange R.

Cape of Good Hope

N

	Areas of Islamic influence
	Trade routes

0   500   1,000 miles

0   500   1,000 kilometers

© maps.com

SOUTH AMERICAN STATES, 500–1532 CE

N

Caribbean Sea

ATLANTIC
OCEAN

ANDES

Quito

Amazon R.

Ucayali R.

CHIMU
800–1465 CE

Chimu

INCA EMPIRE
1438–1532 CE

ANDES

*Machu
Picchu*

Cuzco

Lake Titicaca

Puno
Copacabana
Tiahuanaco

TIAHUANACO
500–1000 CE

Paraguay R.

PACIFIC
OCEAN

San Pedro de Atacama

INCA EMPIRE
1438–1532 CE

ATLANTIC
OCEAN

Coquimbo

Paraná R.

Paraná R.

Talca

0	300	600 miles

0	300	600 kilometers

© maps.com

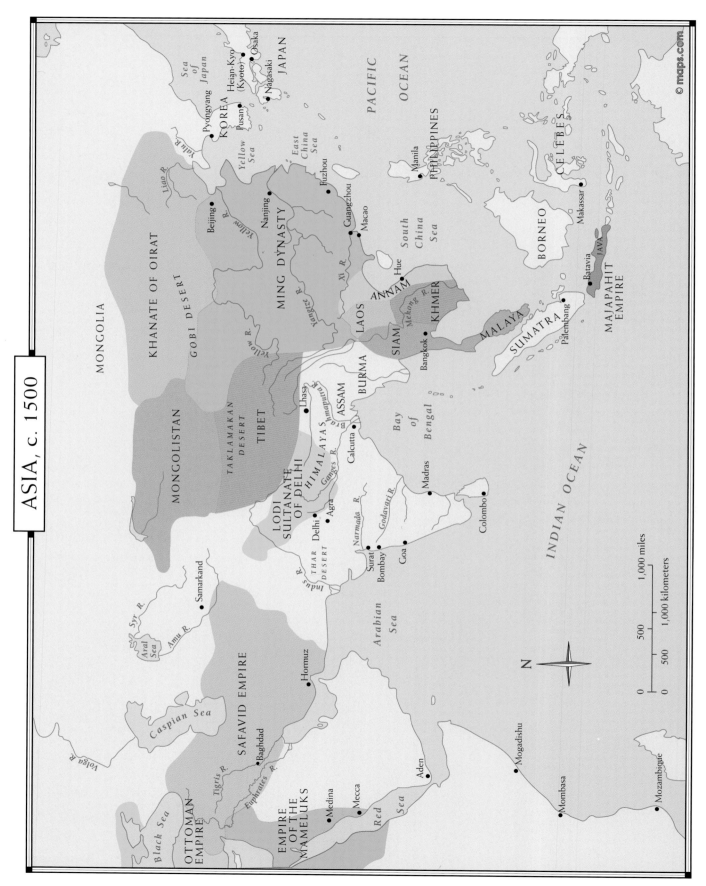

ASIA, c. 1500

MONGOLIA

KHANATE OF OIRAT

GOBI DESERT

MONGOLISTAN

TAKLAMAKAN DESERT

TIBET

MING DYNASTY

KOREA
Pyongyang
Pusan

Sea of Japan
Heian-Kyo (Kyoto)
Osaka
Nagasaki
JAPAN

Yellow Sea

East China Sea

Beijing
Nanjing
Fuzhou
Guangzhou
Macao

Yellow R.
Yangtze
Xi R.

Hue
ANNAM
LAOS
KHMER
SIAM
Bangkok
BURMA

South China Sea

PACIFIC OCEAN

PHILIPPINES
Manila

CELEBES

BORNEO
Makassar

Batavia
JAVA
MAJAPAHIT EMPIRE

MALAYA
SUMATRA
Palembang

Lhasa
HIMALAYAS
ASSAM
Brahmaputra R.
Mekong R.

LODI SULTANATE OF DELHI
THAR DESERT
Delhi
Agra
Ganges R.
Calcutta

Narmada R.
Godavari R.
Surat
Bombay
Goa
Madras
Colombo

Bay of Bengal

INDIAN OCEAN

Indus R.

Samarkand

Syr R.
Amu R.
Aral Sea

SAFAVID EMPIRE
Hormuz

Caspian Sea

Volga R.

Baghdad
Tigris R.
Euphrates R.

OTTOMAN EMPIRE
Black Sea

EMPIRE OF THE MAMELUKS
Medina
Mecca
Red Sea

Arabian Sea

Aden

Mogadishu
Mombasa
Mozambique

Ligao R.
Yalu R.

N

1,000 miles
500
1,000 kilometers
500
0
0

© maps.com

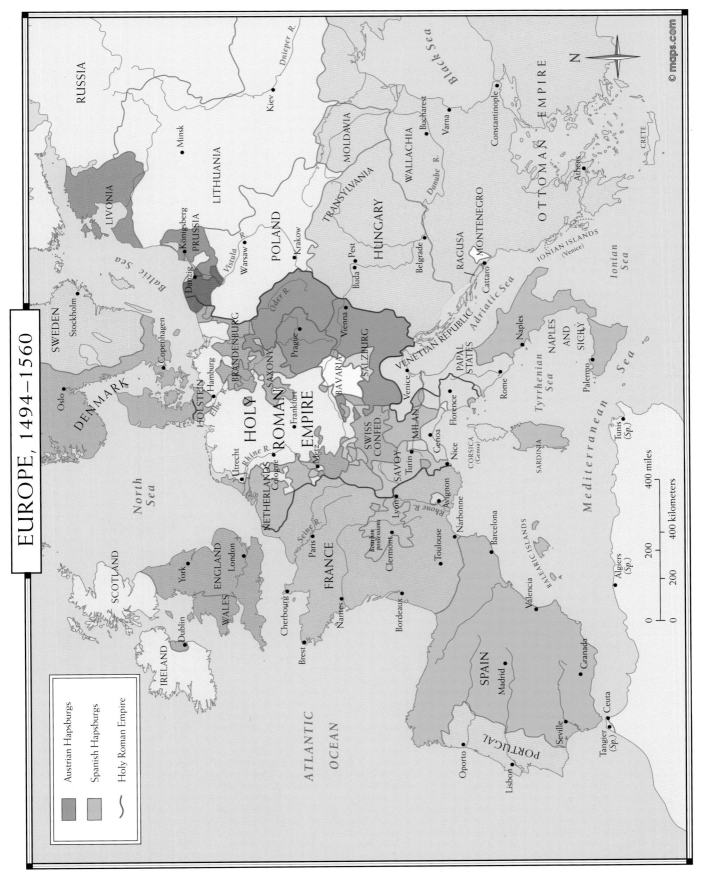

EUROPE, 1494–1560

Legend:
- Austrian Hapsburgs
- Spanish Hapsburgs
- Holy Roman Empire

RUSSIA

SWEDEN

Stockholm

Oslo

DENMARK

Copenhagen

Baltic Sea

LIVONIA

Minsk

LITHUANIA

Kiev

Dnieper R.

PRUSSIA

Königsberg

Danzig

Warsaw

Vistula R.

POLAND

Kraków

MOLDAVIA

Bucharest

Varna

Black Sea

WALLACHIA

Danube R.

TRANSYLVANIA

HUNGARY

Pest

Buda

Belgrade

MONTENEGRO

RAGUSA

Cattaro

Constantinople

OTTOMAN EMPIRE

Athens

CRETE

BRANDENBURG

SAXONY

Oder R.

Prague

Vienna

SALZBURG

BAVARIA

HOLSTEIN

Hamburg

Elbe R.

HOLY ROMAN EMPIRE

Frankfurt

Metz

SWISS CONFED.

VENETIAN REPUBLIC

Venice

Adriatic Sea

IONIAN ISLANDS
(Venice)

Ionian Sea

PAPAL STATES

NAPLES

Naples

NAPLES AND SICILY

Palermo

SICILY

Tyrrhenian Sea

Rome

Florence

Genoa

MILAN

Nice

SAVOY

Turin

CORSICA
(Genoa)

SARDINIA

Mediterranean Sea

Utrecht

NETHERLANDS

Cologne

Rhine R.

SCOTLAND

ENGLAND

York

London

WALES

Dublin

IRELAND

NORTH Sea

Cherbourg

Brest

Nantes

Bordeaux

FRANCE

Paris

Seine R.

Bourbon possessions

Clermont

Lyon

Rhône R.

Avignon

Narbonne

Toulouse

Barcelona

BALEARIC ISLANDS

Valencia

SPAIN

Madrid

Granada

Seville

Oporto

Lisbon

PORTUGAL

Tangier (Sp.)

Ceuta

Algiers (Sp.)

Tunis (Sp.)

ATLANTIC OCEAN

© maps.com

N

400 miles

400 kilometers

200

200

0

0

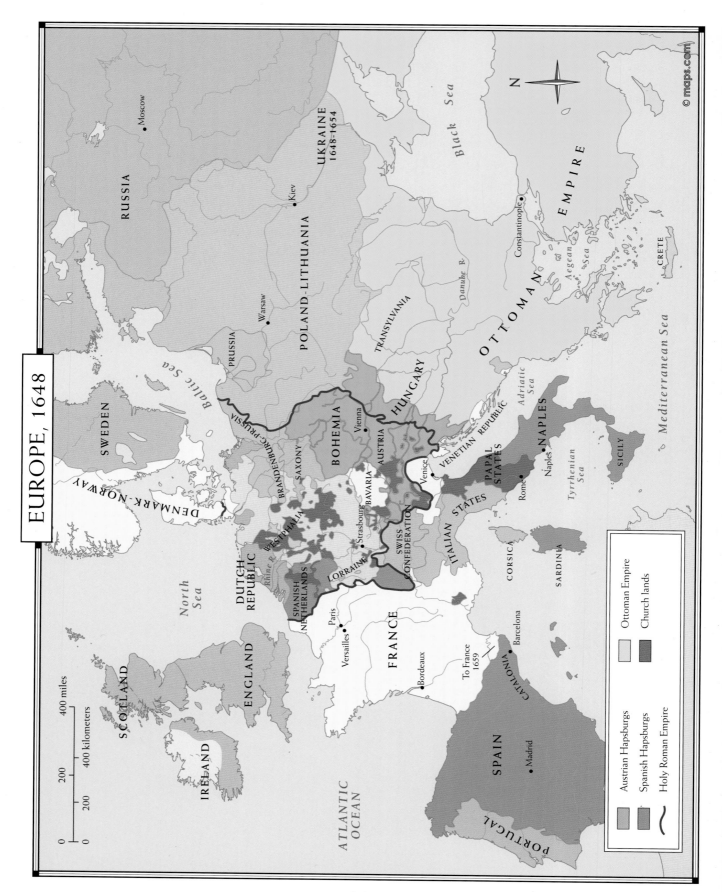

EUROPE, 1648

© maps.com

RUSSIA

Moscow

UKRAINE
1648-1654

Kiev

POLAND-LITHUANIA

Warsaw

PRUSSIA

SWEDEN

DENMARK-NORWAY

NORWAY

Baltic Sea

BRANDENBURG-PRUSSIA

SAXONY

BOHEMIA

Vienna

AUSTRIA

HUNGARY

TRANSYLVANIA

Danube R.

Black Sea

OTTOMAN EMPIRE

Constantinople

Aegean Sea

CRETE

Mediterranean Sea

Adriatic Sea

VENETIAN REPUBLIC

Venice

NAPLES

PAPAL STATES

Rome

Naples

SICILY

Tyrrhenian Sea

CORSICA

SARDINIA

ITALIAN STATES

BAVARIA

SWISS CONFEDERATION

Strasbourg

LORRAINE

WESTPHALIA

Rhine R.

DUTCH REPUBLIC

SPANISH NETHERLANDS

North Sea

SCOTLAND

ENGLAND

IRELAND

400 miles
400 kilometers
200
200
200
0
0

ATLANTIC OCEAN

Paris

Versailles

FRANCE

Bordeaux

To France 1659

Barcelona

CATALONIA

SPAIN

Madrid

PORTUGAL

N

Austrian Hapsburgs

Spanish Hapsburgs

Holy Roman Empire

Ottoman Empire

Church lands

— 24 —

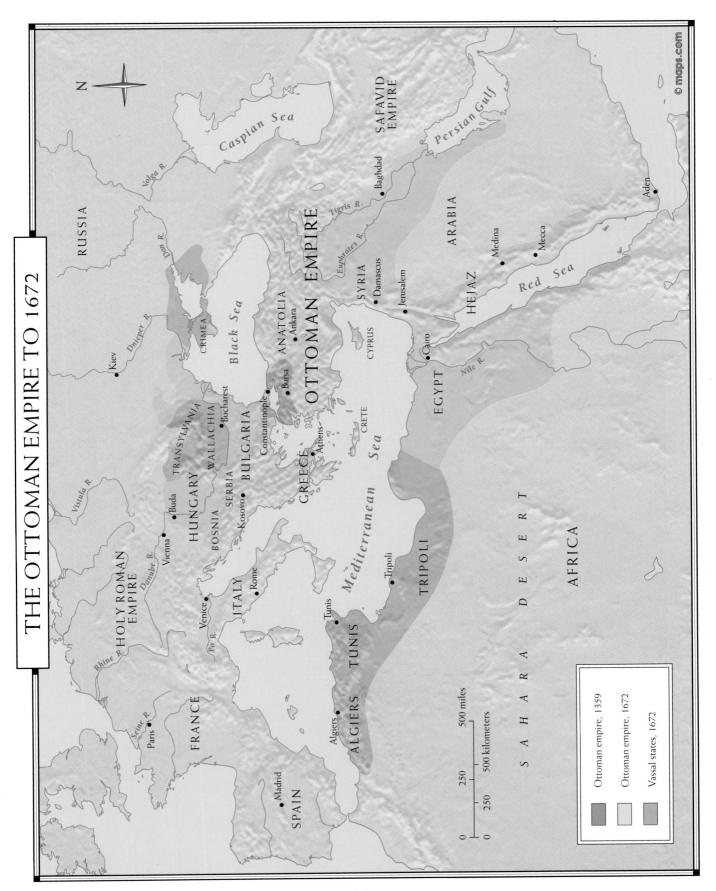

THE OTTOMAN EMPIRE TO 1672

© maps.com

N

RUSSIA

Caspian Sea

Volga R.

Don R.

Dnieper R.

SAFAVID EMPIRE

Persian Gulf

Baghdad

Tigris R.

Euphrates R.

Aden

ARABIA

Medina

Mecca

Red Sea

HEJAZ

Kiev

CRIMEA

Black Sea

ANATOLIA

Ankara

OTTOMAN EMPIRE

SYRIA

Damascus

Jerusalem

Bursa

Constantinople

CYPRUS

Cairo

EGYPT

Nile R.

Bucharest

TRANSYLVANIA

WALLACHIA

BULGARIA

GREECE

Athens

CRETE

Mediterranean Sea

Vistula R.

Buda

HUNGARY

SERBIA

BOSNIA

Kosovo

Vienna

Danube R.

HOLY ROMAN EMPIRE

ITALY

Rome

Venice

Po R.

Rhine R.

Tripoli

TRIPOLI

Seine R.

Paris

FRANCE

Tunis

TUNIS

ALGIERS

Algiers

Madrid

SPAIN

S A H A R A   D E S E R T

A F R I C A

500 miles

500 kilometers

250

500

250

250

0

0

☐	Ottoman empire, 1359
☐	Ottoman empire, 1672
☐	Vassal states, 1672

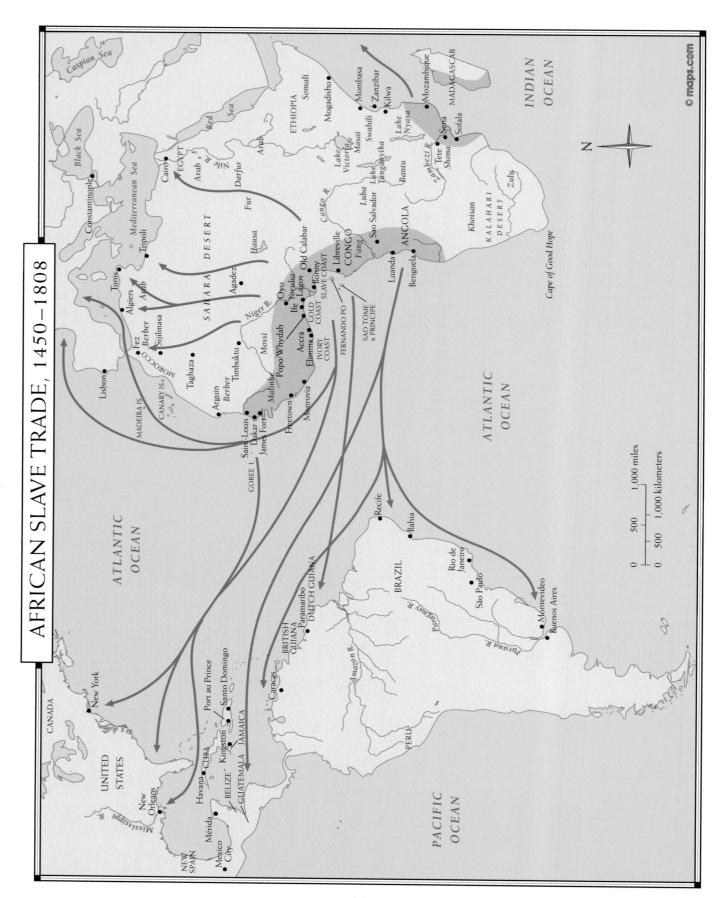

AFRICAN SLAVE TRADE, 1450–1808

© maps.com

INDIAN OCEAN

N

Caspian Sea

Black Sea

Mediterranean Sea

Constantinople

Tripoli

Tunis

Algiers

Fez

Sijilmasa

Berber
Arab

MOROCCO

Taghaza

SAHARA DESERT

Agadez

Hausa

Red Sea

Arab
Nile R.
Darfur
Fur

EGYPT

Cairo

ETHIOPIA

Somali

Mogadishu

Mombasa

Zanzibar

Kilwa

Masai

Swahili

Bantu

Lake Victoria

Lake Tanganyika

Luba

Luba

Mozambique

MADAGASCAR

Sena

Sofala

Zambezi R.

Tete

Shona

Lake Nyasa

Zulu

KALAHARI DESERT

Khoisan

Cape of Good Hope

Niger R.

Timbuktu

Mossi

Malinke

Arguin

Berber

Saint-Louis

Dakar

James Fort

GOREE I.

Freetown

Monrovia

Oyo

Ife

Yoruba

Lagos

Accra

Elmina

Popo/Whydah

GOLD COAST

IVORY COAST

Old Calabar

Bonny

SLAVE COAST

FERNANDO PO

SAO TOME & PRINCIPE

Libreville

CONGO

Fang

Sao Salvador

ANGOLA

Luanda

Benguela

Congo R.

Lisbon

MADEIRA IS.

CANARY IS.

ATLANTIC OCEAN

ATLANTIC OCEAN

PACIFIC OCEAN

CANADA

UNITED STATES

New York

New Orleans

Mississippi R.

NEW SPAIN

Mexico City

Mérida

Havana

CUBA

BELIZE

GUATEMALA

Port au Prince

Santo Domingo

Kingston

JAMAICA

Caracas

BRITISH GUIANA

Paramaribo

DUTCH GUIANA

Amazon R.

PERU

BRAZIL

Recife

Bahia

Rio de Janeiro

São Paulo

Paraguay R.

Paraná R.

Montevideo

Buenos Aires

1,000 miles

500

0

1,000 kilometers

500

0

– 26 –

EXPLORATION AND COLONIZATION, c. 1700

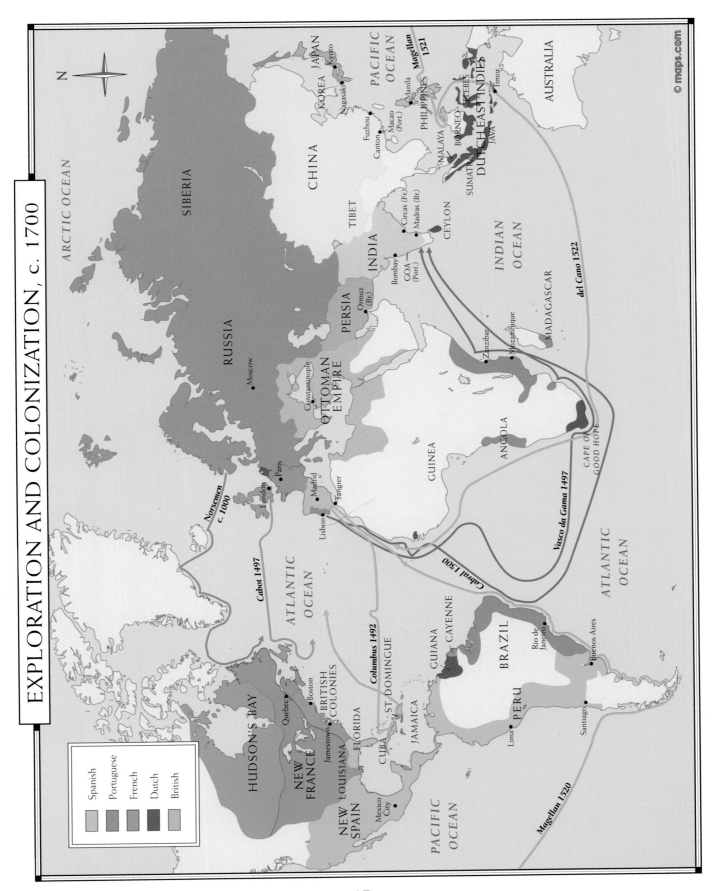

Legend:
- Spanish
- Portuguese
- French
- Dutch
- British

ARCTIC OCEAN

SIBERIA

RUSSIA

Moscow

CHINA

KOREA JAPAN
Kyoto
Nagasaki

PACIFIC OCEAN

Magellan 1521

Manila

PHILIPPINES

Fuzhou
Canton
Macao (Port.)

MALAYA

BORNEO CELEBES

DUTCH EAST INDIES

SUMATRA

JAVA

Timor

AUSTRALIA

TIBET

Circas (Fr)
Madras (Br)

CEYLON

Bombay
GOA (Port.)

INDIA

INDIAN OCEAN

MADAGASCAR

PERSIA

Ormuz (Br)

OTTOMAN EMPIRE

Constantinople

del Cano 1522

Zanzibar
Mozambique

GUINEA

ANGOLA

Paris

London
Norsemen c. 1000

Madrid

Tangier

Lisbon

Cabot 1497

ATLANTIC OCEAN

CAPE OF GOOD HOPE

Vasco da Gama 1497

Cabral 1500

Columbus 1492

ATLANTIC OCEAN

GUIANA
CAYENNE

BRAZIL

Rio de Janeiro

Buenos Aires

PERU

Lima

Santiago

Magellan 1520

PACIFIC OCEAN

HUDSON'S BAY

NEW FRANCE

Quebec
Boston
BRITISH COLONIES
Jamestown
FLORIDA

NEW LOUISIANA

CUBA
ST. DOMINGUE
JAMAICA

NEW SPAIN

Mexico City

N

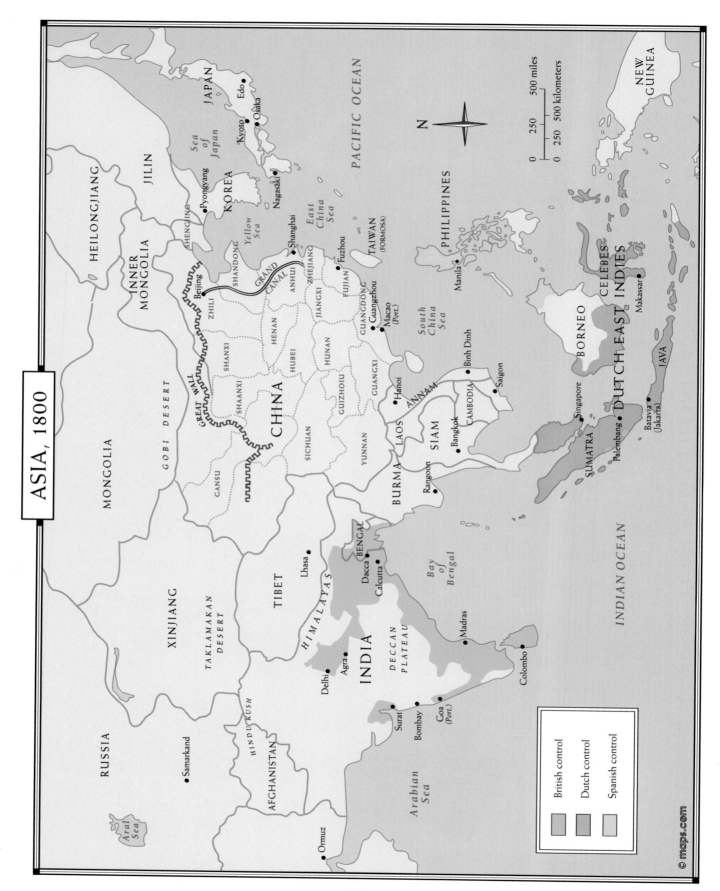

ASIA, 1800

RUSSIA

HEILONGJIANG

MONGOLIA

INNER
MONGOLIA

JILIN

SHENGJING

KOREA

Pyongyang

JAPAN

Edo

Kyoto
Osaka

Sea
of
Japan

Nagasaki

GOBI DESERT

XINJIANG

TAKLAMAKAN
DESERT

GANSU

GREAT WALL

Beijing
ZHILI

SHANDONG

Yellow
Sea

SHANXI

SHAANXI

HENAN

HUBEI

GRAND CANAL

Shanghai

ANHUI

ZHEJIANG

Fuzhou
FUJIAN

East
China
Sea

TAIWAN
(FORMOSA)

PACIFIC OCEAN

PHILIPPINES

Manila

500 miles

500 kilometers

250

250   500

0

0

N

NEW
GUINEA

CHINA

SICHUAN

GUIZHOU

HUNAN

JIANGXI

GUANGXI

GUANGDONG

Guangzhou
Macao
(Port.)

South
China
Sea

BORNEO

CELEBES

Makassar

DUTCH EAST INDIES

TIBET

Lhasa

HIMALAYAS

YUNNAN

BURMA

LAOS

Hanoi

ANNAM

Binh Dinh

SIAM

Bangkok

CAMBODIA

Saigon

Rangoon

Singapore

SUMATRA

Palembang

JAVA

Batavia
(Jakarta)

AFGHANISTAN

HINDU KUSH

Samarkand

Aral
Sea

Ormuz

BENGAL

Dacca

Calcutta

Bay
of
Bengal

INDIA

DECCAN
PLATEAU

Madras

Colombo

INDIAN OCEAN

Delhi

Agra

Surat

Bombay

Goa
(Port.)

Arabian
Sea

British control

Dutch control

Spanish control

© maps.com

— 28 —

DECLINE OF THE OTTOMAN EMPIRE, 1774–1914

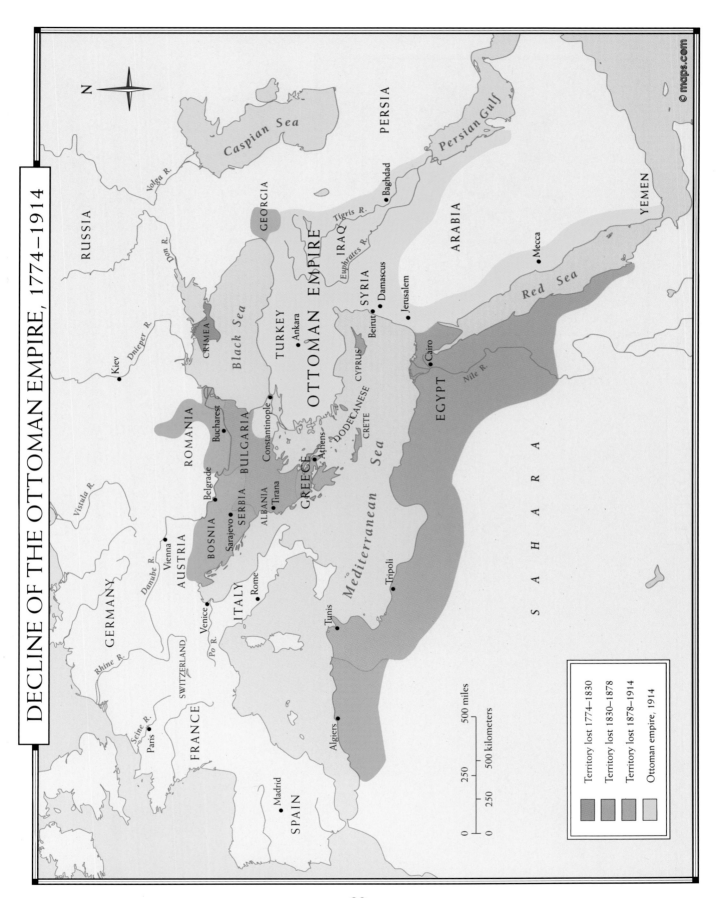

© maps.com

RUSSIA

Caspian Sea

Volga R.

Don R.

Dnieper R.

Kiev

PERSIA

Persian Gulf

GEORGIA

Baghdad

Tigris R.

ARABIA

YEMEN

TURKEY

Ankara

OTTOMAN EMPIRE

IRAQ

Euphrates R.

SYRIA

Damascus

Jerusalem

Beirut

Mecca

Red Sea

Black Sea

CRIMEA

ROMANIA

Bucharest

Belgrade

BULGARIA

Constantinople

SERBIA

Athens

GREECE

CYPRUS

DODECANESE

CRETE

Cairo

EGYPT

Nile R.

BOSNIA

Sarajevo

ALBANIA

Tirana

Mediterranean Sea

S A H A R A

AUSTRIA

Vienna

Danube R.

Vistula R.

ITALY

Rome

Venice

Po R.

Tripoli

Tunis

Algiers

GERMANY

Rhine R.

SWITZERLAND

FRANCE

Seine R.

Paris

Madrid

SPAIN

N

Legend:
- Territory lost 1774–1830
- Territory lost 1830–1878
- Territory lost 1878–1914
- Ottoman empire, 1914

500 miles

250

0

500 kilometers

250

0

EUROPE, 1815

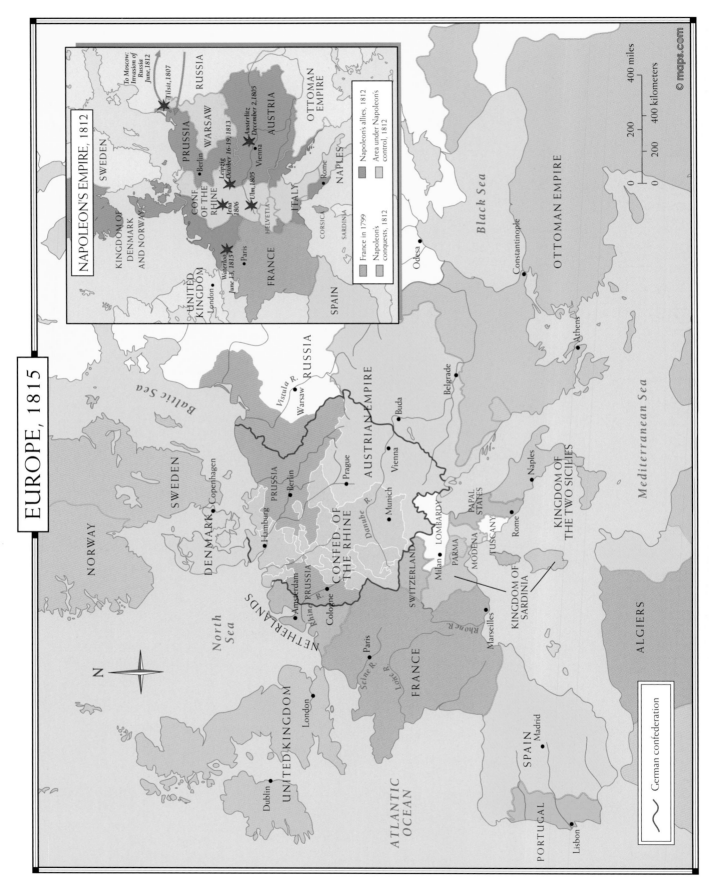

NAPOLEON'S EMPIRE, 1812

SWEDEN

RUSSIA

To Moscow: Invasion of Russia June, 1812

Tilsit, 1807

PRUSSIA

WARSAW

KINGDOM OF DENMARK AND NORWAY

Berlin

Leipzig October 16-19, 1813

CONF. OF THE RHINE

Jena 1806

Ulm, 1805

AUSTRIA

Vienna

Austerlitz December 2, 1805

OTTOMAN EMPIRE

HELVETIA

ITALY

Rome

NAPLES

Waterloo June 18, 1815

UNITED KINGDOM

London

FRANCE

Paris

CORSICA

SARDINIA

SPAIN

France in 1799

Napoleon's conquests, 1812

Napoleon's allies, 1812

Area under Napoleon's control, 1812

© maps.com

400 miles

400 kilometers

0   200

0   200

Black Sea

Odesa

Constantinople

OTTOMAN EMPIRE

Athens

Mediterranean Sea

NORWAY

SWEDEN

Baltic Sea

RUSSIA

Vistula R.

Warsaw

DENMARK

Copenhagen

North Sea

PRUSSIA

Berlin

Hamburg

PRUSSIA

CONFED. OF THE RHINE

Danube R.

Prague

Munich

AUSTRIAN EMPIRE

Buda

Vienna

Belgrade

NETHERLANDS

Amsterdam

Rhine R.

Cologne

SWITZERLAND

LOMBARDY

Milan

PARMA

MODENA

PAPAL STATES

TUSCANY

Rome

KINGDOM OF SARDINIA

KINGDOM OF THE TWO SICILIES

Naples

UNITED KINGDOM

Dublin

London

ATLANTIC OCEAN

Seine R.

Paris

Loire R.

FRANCE

Rhone R.

Marseilles

ALGIERS

SPAIN

Madrid

PORTUGAL

Lisbon

N

German confederation

LATIN AMERICAN INDEPENDENCE, 19th CENTURY

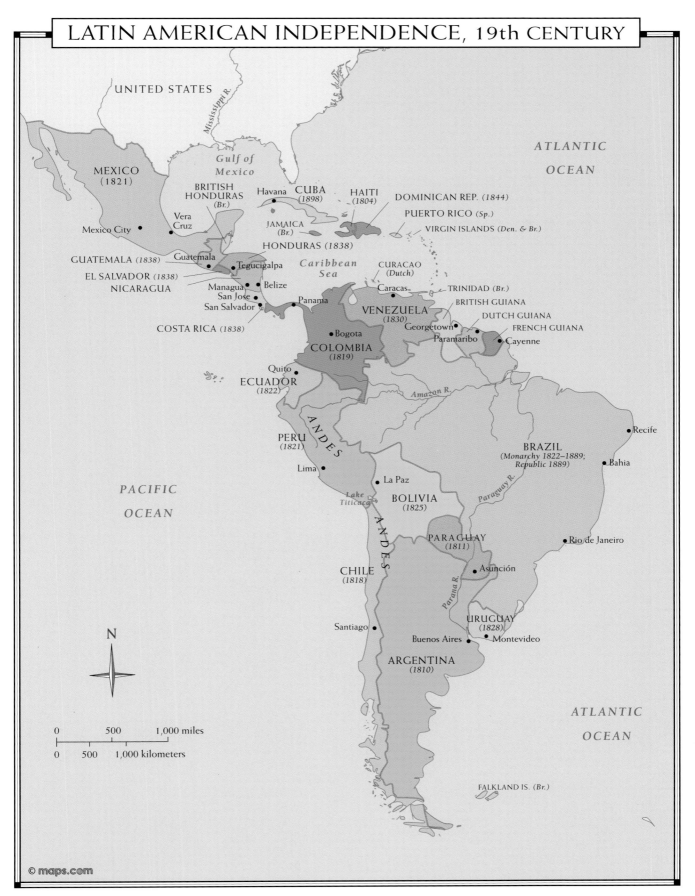

UNITED STATES

Mississippi R.

Gulf of Mexico

ATLANTIC OCEAN

MEXICO (1821)

BRITISH HONDURAS *(Br.)*

Havana

CUBA *(1898)*

HAITI *(1804)*

DOMINICAN REP. *(1844)*

PUERTO RICO *(Sp.)*

VIRGIN ISLANDS *(Den. & Br.)*

Vera Cruz

Mexico City

JAMAICA *(Br.)*

HONDURAS *(1838)*

GUATEMALA *(1838)*

Guatemala

Tegucigalpa

Caribbean Sea

CURACAO *(Dutch)*

EL SALVADOR *(1838)*

NICARAGUA

Managua

Belize

San Jose

San Salvador

Panama

Caracas

TRINIDAD *(Br.)*

VENEZUELA *(1830)*

BRITISH GUIANA

DUTCH GUIANA

Georgetown

Paramaribo

FRENCH GUIANA

Cayenne

COSTA RICA *(1838)*

Bogota

COLOMBIA *(1819)*

Quito

ECUADOR *(1822)*

Amazon R.

ANDES

PERU *(1821)*

Lima

Recife

BRAZIL
*Monarchy 1822–1889;
Republic 1889*

Bahia

La Paz

Lake Titicaca

BOLIVIA *(1825)*

Paraguay R.

PACIFIC OCEAN

PARAGUAY *(1811)*

Rio de Janeiro

ANDES

CHILE *(1818)*

Asunción

Parana R.

URUGUAY *(1828)*

Santiago

Buenos Aires

Montevideo

N

ARGENTINA *(1810)*

ATLANTIC OCEAN

0   500   1,000 miles

0   500   1,000 kilometers

FALKLAND IS. *(Br.)*

© maps.com

INDUSTRIALIZATION AND URBANIZATION IN EUROPE, c. 1850

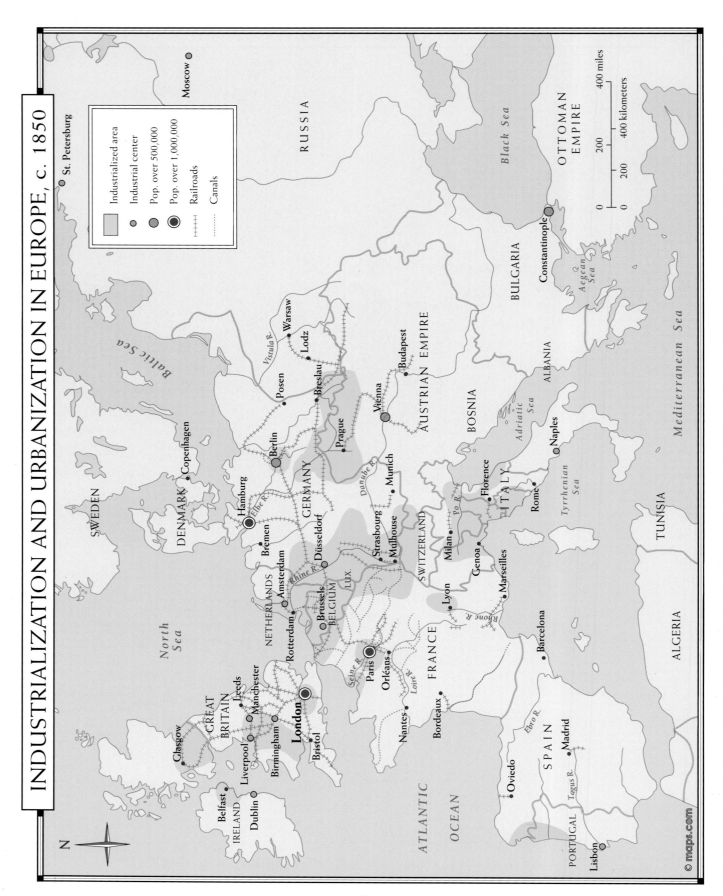

Legend:
- Industrialized area
- Industrial center
- Pop. over 500,000
- Pop. over 1,000,000
- Railroads
- Canals

400 miles
400 kilometers
200
0
200
0

RUSSIA

Moscow

St. Petersburg

OTTOMAN EMPIRE

Black Sea

Constantinople

Aegean Sea

BULGARIA

ALBANIA

BOSNIA

Adriatic Sea

AUSTRIAN EMPIRE

Budapest

Vienna

Warsaw

Lodz

Posen

Breslau

Prague

Berlin

Vistula R.

Baltic Sea

Copenhagen

DENMARK

SWEDEN

Hamburg

Elbe R.

Bremen

GERMANY

Danube R.

Munich

Strasbourg

Mulhouse

Düsseldorf

Rhine R.

Amsterdam

NETHERLANDS

Rotterdam

Brussels

BELGIUM

LUX.

SWITZERLAND

Milan

Genoa

Florence

Po R.

ITALY

Rome

Naples

Tyrrhenian Sea

Mediterranean Sea

TUNISIA

ALGERIA

Marseilles

Lyon

Rhône R.

Paris

Seine R.

Orléans

Loire R.

FRANCE

Nantes

Bordeaux

Barcelona

Madrid

Ebro R.

SPAIN

Oviedo

Tagus R.

PORTUGAL

Lisbon

North Sea

ATLANTIC OCEAN

GREAT BRITAIN

Leeds

Manchester

Liverpool

Birmingham

Glasgow

Bristol

London

Belfast

IRELAND

Dublin

N

© maps.com

- 32 -

IMPERIALISM IN THE MODERN WORLD, 1900

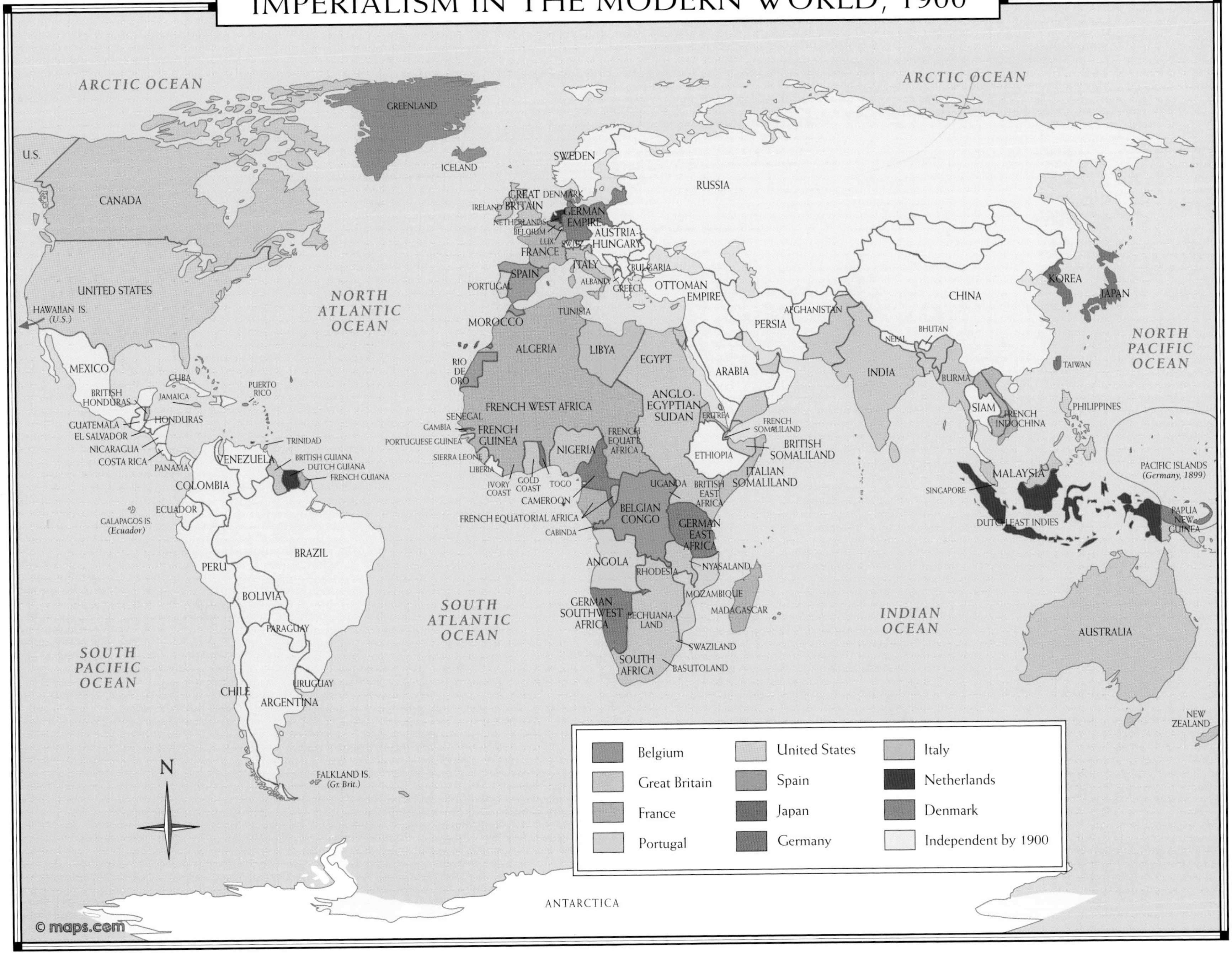

Legend

Belgium	Italy
Great Britain	Netherlands
France	Denmark
Portugal	Independent by 1900
United States	
Spain	
Japan	
Germany	

Oceans and regions:
ARCTIC OCEAN · NORTH PACIFIC OCEAN · NORTH ATLANTIC OCEAN · SOUTH ATLANTIC OCEAN · SOUTH PACIFIC OCEAN · INDIAN OCEAN · ANTARCTICA

Labels:

NEW ZEALAND · PACIFIC ISLANDS (Germany, 1899) · PAPUA NEW GUINEA · AUSTRALIA · JAPAN · KOREA · TAIWAN · PHILIPPINES · FRENCH INDOCHINA · SIAM · BURMA · CHINA · MALAYSIA · DUTCH EAST INDIES · SINGAPORE · BHUTAN · NEPAL · INDIA · AFGHANISTAN · PERSIA · ARABIA · RUSSIA · OTTOMAN EMPIRE · SWEDEN · DENMARK · GERMAN EMPIRE · NETHERLANDS · BELGIUM · LUX. · GREAT BRITAIN · IRELAND · FRANCE · SPAIN · PORTUGAL · AUSTRIA-HUNGARY · ITALY · ALBANIA · GREECE · BULGARIA · SERVIA · ICELAND · GREENLAND

EGYPT · ANGLO-EGYPTIAN SUDAN · LIBYA · TUNISIA · MOROCCO · ALGERIA · RIO DE ORO · SENEGAL · GAMBIA · PORTUGUESE GUINEA · FRENCH WEST AFRICA · FRENCH GUINEA · SIERRA LEONE · LIBERIA · IVORY COAST · GOLD COAST · TOGO · NIGERIA · CAMEROON · FRENCH EQUATORIAL AFRICA · CABINDA · ERITREA · FRENCH SOMALILAND · BRITISH SOMALILAND · ITALIAN SOMALILAND · ETHIOPIA · UGANDA · BRITISH EAST AFRICA · GERMAN EAST AFRICA · BELGIAN CONGO · FRENCH EQUATORIAL AFRICA · ANGOLA · NYASALAND · MOZAMBIQUE · MADAGASCAR · RHODESIA · GERMAN SOUTH-WEST AFRICA · BECHUANALAND · SWAZILAND · SOUTH AFRICA · BASUTOLAND

CANADA · UNITED STATES · U.S. · HAWAIIAN IS. (U.S.) · MEXICO · BRITISH HONDURAS · GUATEMALA · EL SALVADOR · HONDURAS · NICARAGUA · COSTA RICA · PANAMA · CUBA · JAMAICA · PUERTO RICO · TRINIDAD · VENEZUELA · COLOMBIA · ECUADOR · GALAPAGOS IS. (Ecuador) · PERU · BOLIVIA · BRAZIL · BRITISH GUIANA · DUTCH GUIANA · FRENCH GUIANA · PARAGUAY · URUGUAY · CHILE · ARGENTINA · FALKLAND IS. (Gt. Brit.)

N

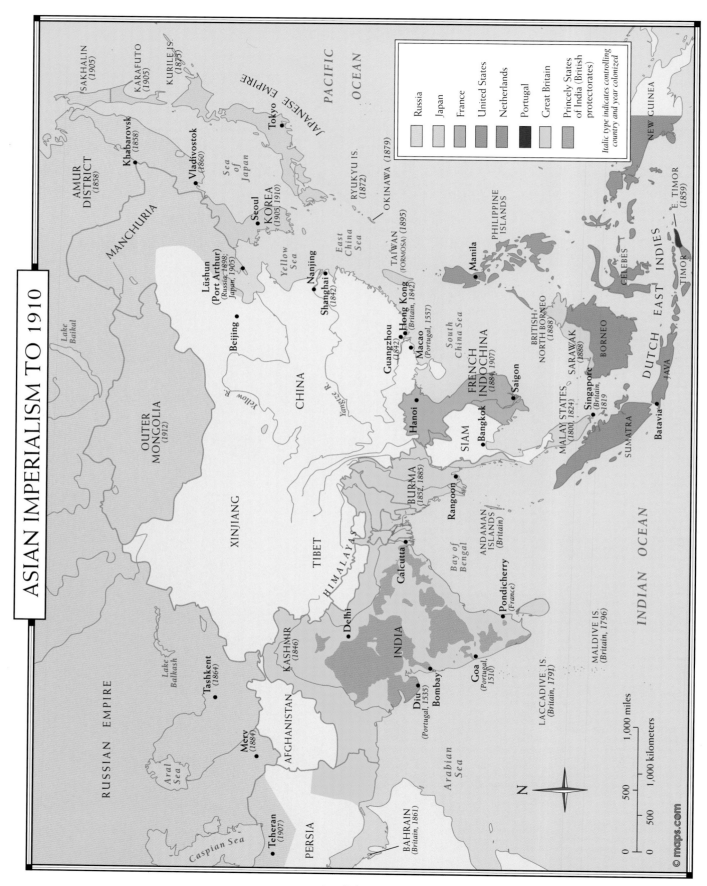

ASIAN IMPERIALISM TO 1910

Legend:
- Russia
- Japan
- France
- United States
- Netherlands
- Portugal
- Great Britain
- Princely States of India (British protectorates)

Italic type indicates controlling country and year colonized

RUSSIAN EMPIRE

SAKHALIN (1905)
KARAFUTO (1905)
KURILE IS. (1875)

PACIFIC OCEAN

JAPANESE EMPIRE

Tokyo

Sea of Japan

Khabarovsk (1858)
Vladivostok (1860)

AMUR DISTRICT (1858)

MANCHURIA

Seoul (1905) KOREA (1905, 1910)

RYUKYU IS. (1872)
OKINAWA (1879)

Lüshun (Port Arthur) (Russia, 1898; Japan, 1905)

Yellow Sea

Nanjing (1842)

East China Sea

TAIWAN (FORMOSA) (1895)

PHILIPPINE ISLANDS

Manila

Lake Baikal

OUTER MONGOLIA (1912)

Beijing

Shanghai (1842)

CHINA

Yellow R.

Yangtze R.

Guangzhou (1842)
Hong Kong (Britain, 1842)
Macao (Portugal, 1557)

South China Sea

CELEBES

E. TIMOR (1859)

TIMOR

NEW GUINEA

XINJIANG

TIBET

HIMALAYAS

FRENCH INDOCHINA (1884, 1907)

Hanoi

SIAM
Bangkok

Saigon

BRITISH NORTH BORNEO (1888)

SARAWAK (1888)

BORNEO

DUTCH EAST INDIES

Singapore (Britain, 1819)

MALAY STATES (1800, 1824)

SUMATRA

JAVA

Batavia

Tashkent (1864)

Lake Balkhash

Aral Sea

KASHMIR (1846)

AFGHANISTAN

Merv (1884)

BURMA (1852, 1885)

Rangoon

Calcutta

INDIA

Delhi

ANDAMAN ISLANDS (Britain)

Bay of Bengal

Pondicherry (France)

Diu (Portugal, 1535)
Bombay

Goa (Portugal, 1510)

MALDIVE IS. (Britain, 1796)

LACCADIVE IS. (Britain, 1791)

INDIAN OCEAN

Arabian Sea

Teheran (1907)

PERSIA

BAHRAIN (Britain, 1861)

Caspian Sea

1,000 miles
1,000 kilometers
500
1,000
500
500
0
0

N

© maps.com

— 34 —

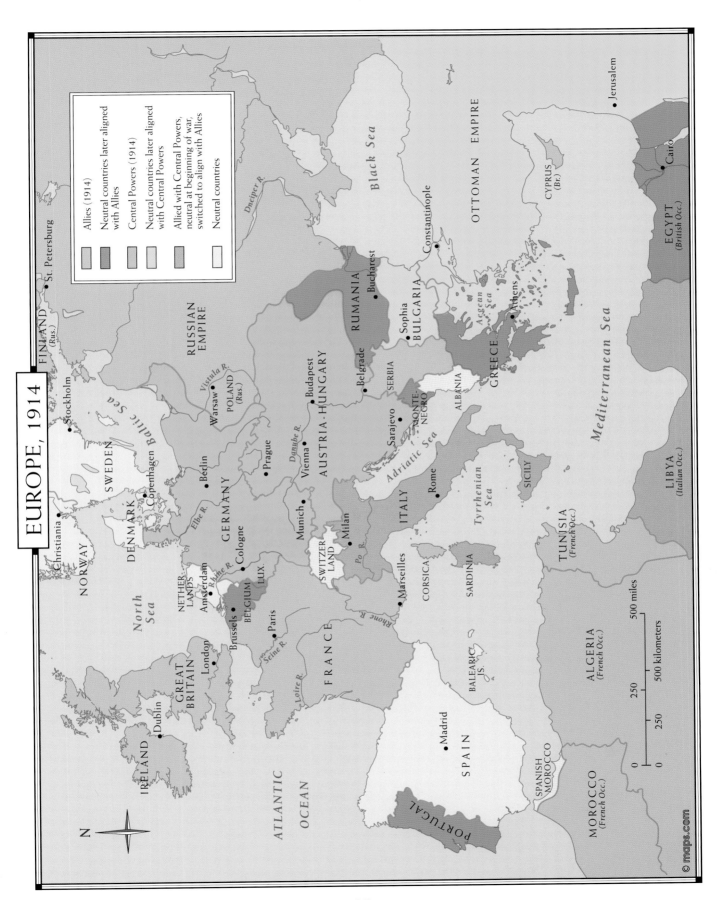

EUROPE, 1914

Legend:
- Allies (1914)
- Neutral countries later aligned with Allies
- Central Powers (1914)
- Neutral countries later aligned with Central Powers
- Allied with Central Powers, neutral at beginning of war, switched to align with Allies
- Neutral countries

N

FINLAND (Rus.)
· St. Petersburg

NORWAY
· Christiania

SWEDEN
· Stockholm

Baltic Sea

DENMARK
· Copenhagen

North Sea

IRELAND
· Dublin

GREAT BRITAIN
· London

ATLANTIC OCEAN

NETHER-LANDS
· Amsterdam

BELGIUM
· Brussels

LUX.

FRANCE
· Paris

Seine R.
Loire R.
Rhône R.

GERMANY
· Berlin
· Cologne
· Munich

Elbe R.
Rhine R.

POLAND (Rus.)
· Warsaw

Vistula R.

RUSSIAN EMPIRE

Dnieper R.

Prague ·

AUSTRIA-HUNGARY
· Vienna
· Budapest

Danube R.

SWITZER-LAND

ITALY
· Milan
· Rome

Po R.

· Marseilles

CORSICA

SARDINIA

Tyrrhenian Sea

SICILY

Adriatic Sea

SERBIA
· Belgrade
· Sarajevo

MONTE-NEGRO

ALBANIA

RUMANIA
· Bucharest

BULGARIA
· Sophia

Black Sea

GREECE
· Athens

Aegean Sea

Constantinople ·

OTTOMAN EMPIRE

CYPRUS (Br.)

Mediterranean Sea

EGYPT (British Occ.)
· Cairo

· Jerusalem

LIBYA (Italian Occ.)

TUNISIA (French Occ.)

ALGERIA (French Occ.)

SPAIN
· Madrid

BALEARIC IS.

PORTUGAL

SPANISH MOROCCO

MOROCCO (French Occ.)

500 miles
0   250   500 kilometers
0   250

© maps.com

AFRICA, 1914

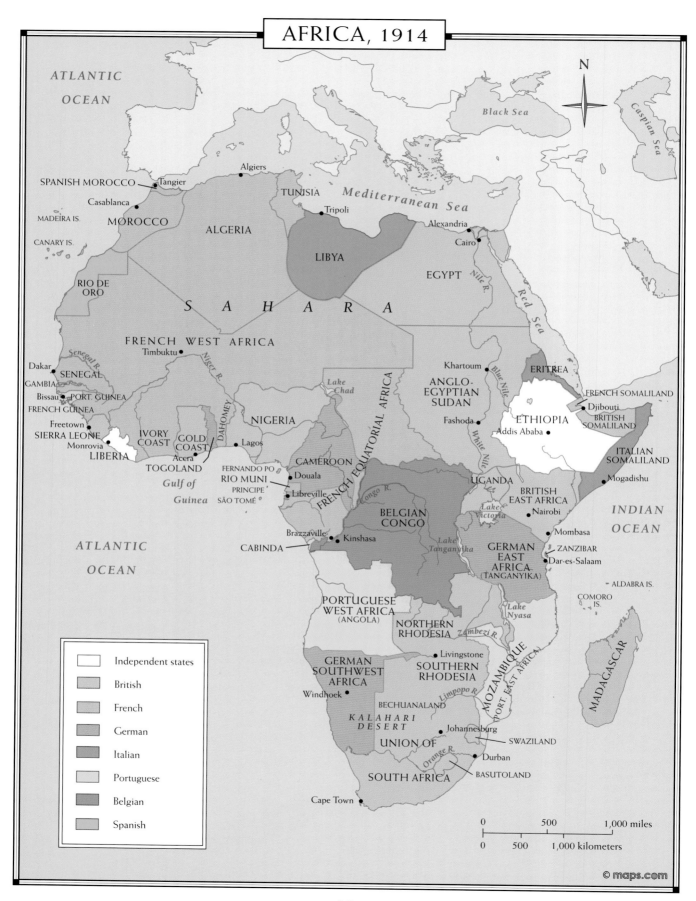

ATLANTIC OCEAN

Black Sea

N

Caspian Sea

SPANISH MOROCCO • Tangier
Algiers
TUNISIA
Mediterranean Sea

Casablanca

MADEIRA IS.

MOROCCO
ALGERIA
• Tripoli
Alexandria •
• Cairo

CANARY IS.

LIBYA
EGYPT

RIO DE ORO

Red Sea

Nile R.

S A H A R A

FRENCH WEST AFRICA
• Timbuktu

Khartoum •
ANGLO-EGYPTIAN SUDAN
ERITREA

Senegal R.

Niger R.

FRENCH SOMALILAND

Dakar •
SENEGAL

Lake Chad

Blue Nile

GAMBIA
Bissau • PORT. GUINEA
FRENCH GUINEA

Fashoda •
ETHIOPIA
• Djibouti
BRITISH SOMALILAND

Freetown •
SIERRA LEONE
Monrovia •
LIBERIA

IVORY COAST
GOLD COAST
Acera •
NIGERIA
• Lagos

White Nile
Addis Ababa •

ITALIAN SOMALILAND

DAHOMEY
TOGOLAND
Gulf of Guinea

CAMEROON

UGANDA
BRITISH EAST AFRICA

• Mogadishu

FERNANDO PO
RIO MUNI
PRINCIPE
SÃO TOMÉ

• Douala
• Libreville

FRENCH EQUATORIAL AFRICA

Congo R.

BELGIAN CONGO

Lake Victoria
Nairobi •

INDIAN OCEAN

ATLANTIC OCEAN

Brazzaville •
• Kinshasa
CABINDA

Lake Tanganyika

GERMAN EAST AFRICA (TANGANYIKA)

• Mombasa

ZANZIBAR
Dar-es-Salaam •

— ALDABRA IS.

PORTUGUESE WEST AFRICA (ANGOLA)

Lake Nyasa

COMORO IS.

NORTHERN RHODESIA
Zambezi R.

GERMAN SOUTHWEST AFRICA
• Livingstone
SOUTHERN RHODESIA

MOZAMBIQUE (PORT. EAST AFRICA)

MADAGASCAR

Windhoek •

BECHUANALAND

Limpopo R.

KALAHARI DESERT

• Johannesburg
SWAZILAND

UNION OF SOUTH AFRICA
Orange R.
• Durban
BASUTOLAND

Cape Town •

Legend

☐	Independent states
▨	British
▨	French
▨	German
▨	Italian
☐	Portuguese
▨	Belgian
▨	Spanish

0 ___ 500 ___ 1,000 miles
0 ___ 500 ___ 1,000 kilometers

© maps.com

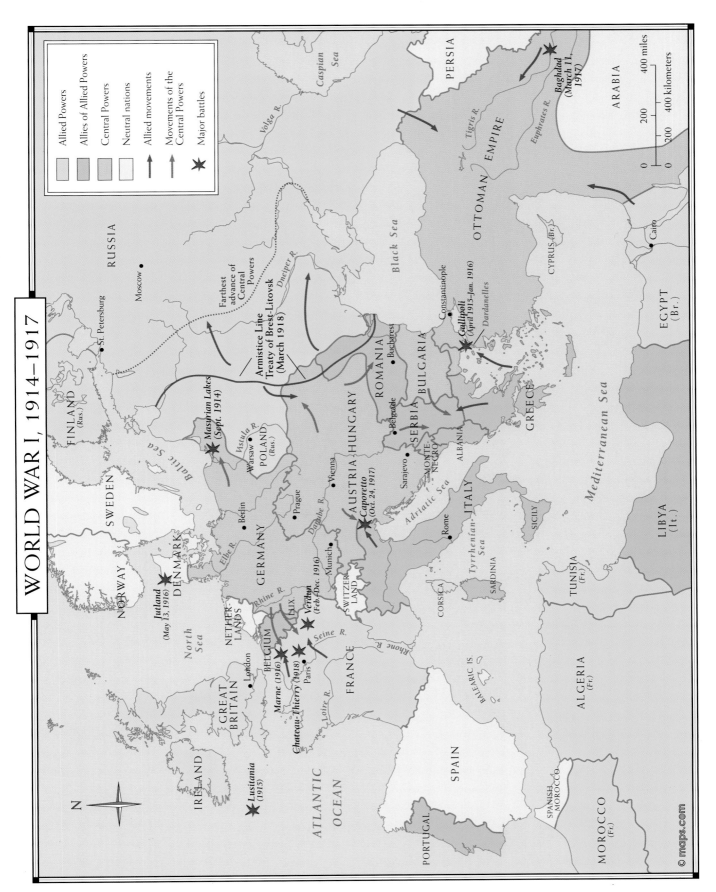

WORLD WAR I, 1914–1917

Legend:
- Allied Powers
- Allies of Allied Powers
- Central Powers
- Neutral nations
- Allied movements
- Movements of the Central Powers
- Major battles

Labels on map:

RUSSIA
FINLAND (Rus.)
SWEDEN
NORWAY
DENMARK
GREAT BRITAIN
IRELAND
NETHERLANDS
BELGIUM
LUX.
FRANCE
GERMANY
POLAND (Rus.)
SWITZERLAND
AUSTRIA-HUNGARY
ITALY
SERBIA
BULGARIA
ROMANIA
MONTENEGRO
ALBANIA
GREECE
SPAIN
PORTUGAL
SPANISH MOROCCO
MOROCCO (Fr.)
ALGERIA (Fr.)
TUNISIA (Fr.)
LIBYA (It.)
EGYPT (Br.)
ARABIA
OTTOMAN EMPIRE
PERSIA
CYPRUS (Br.)

St. Petersburg
Moscow
Warsaw
Berlin
Prague
Vienna
Munich
Paris
London
Rome
Belgrade
Sarajevo
Bucharest
Constantinople
Cairo

Seas and rivers:
Caspian Sea
Black Sea
Baltic Sea
North Sea
ATLANTIC OCEAN
Mediterranean Sea
Adriatic Sea
Tyrrhenian Sea
Volga R.
Dnieper R.
Vistula R.
Elbe R.
Rhine R.
Danube R.
Seine R.
Loire R.
Rhône R.
Tigris R.
Euphrates R.

Islands:
SICILY
SARDINIA
CORSICA
BALEARIC IS.

Battles and events:
- Lusitania (1915)
- Jutland (May 13, 1916)
- Masurian Lakes (Sept. 1914)
- Marne (1916)
- Château-Thierry (1918)
- Verdun (Feb.–Dec. 1916)
- Caporetto (Oct. 24, 1917)
- Gallipoli (April 1915–Jan. 1916)
- Dardanelles
- Baghdad (March 11, 1917)

Annotations:
- Farthest advance of Central Powers
- Armistice Line Treaty of Brest-Litovsk (March 1918)

© maps.com

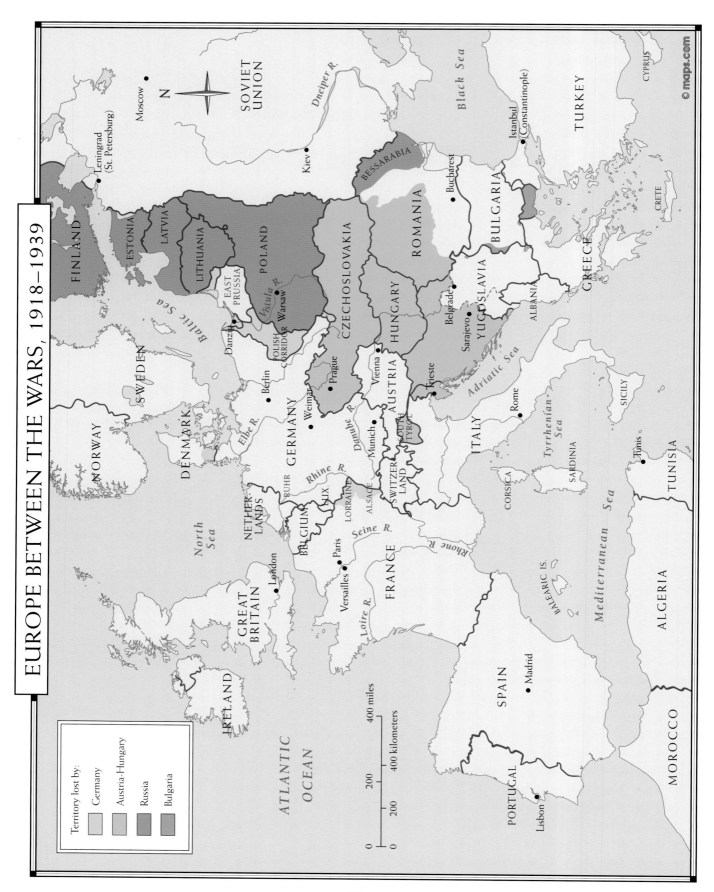

EUROPE BETWEEN THE WARS, 1918–1939

Territory lost by:
- Germany
- Austria-Hungary
- Russia
- Bulgaria

SOVIET UNION

Moscow

Dneiper R.

Black Sea

CYPRUS

TURKEY

Istanbul (Constantinople)

CRETE

GREECE

Leningrad (St. Petersburg)

Kiev

BESSARABIA

Bucharest

BULGARIA

FINLAND

ESTONIA

LATVIA

LITHUANIA

POLAND

ROMANIA

EAST PRUSSIA

Vistula R.

Warsaw

CZECHOSLOVAKIA

HUNGARY

YUGOSLAVIA

ALBANIA

Baltic Sea

Danzig

POLISH CORRIDOR

Belgrade

Sarajevo

Adriatic Sea

SWEDEN

Berlin

Prague

Vienna

AUSTRIA

Trieste

Weimar

GERMANY

Elbe R.

Danube R.

Munich

SOUTH TYROL

Rome

SICILY

NORWAY

DENMARK

Tyrrhenian Sea

SARDINIA

Tunis

TUNISIA

RUHR

Rhine R.

ITALY

North Sea

NETHER-LANDS

LUX.

LORRAINE

ALSACE

SWITZER-LAND

CORSICA

Mediterranean Sea

BELGIUM

London

Paris

Seine R.

FRANCE

BALEARIC IS.

ALGERIA

GREAT BRITAIN

Versailles

Loire R.

Rhone R.

IRELAND

ATLANTIC OCEAN

SPAIN

Madrid

400 miles

400 kilometers

200

200

PORTUGAL

Lisbon

MOROCCO

© maps.com

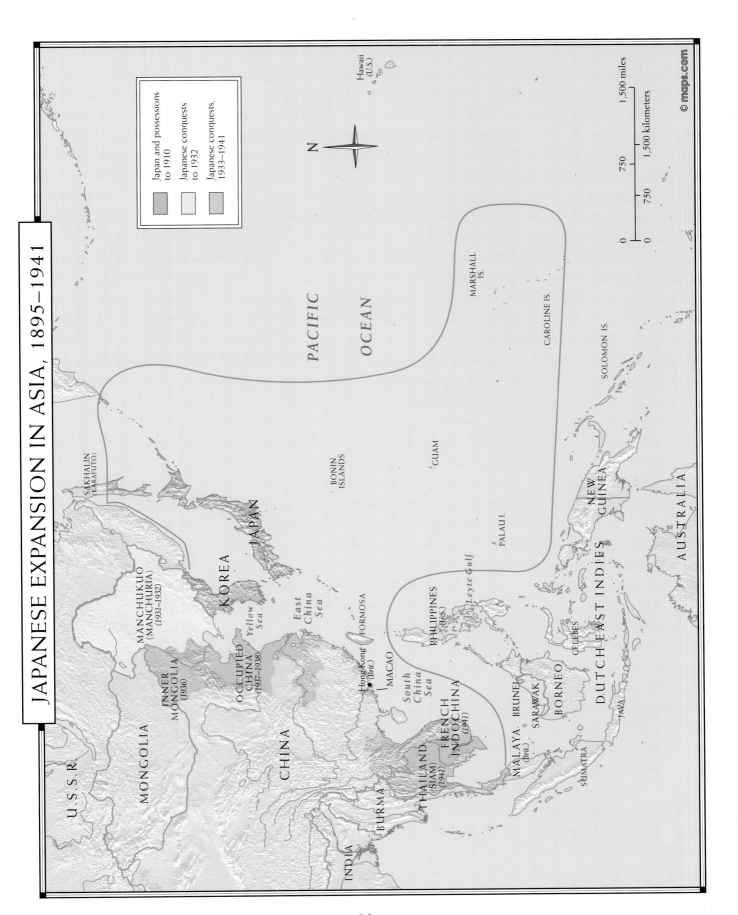

JAPANESE EXPANSION IN ASIA, 1895–1941

Japan and possessions to 1910

Japanese conquests to 1932

Japanese conquests, 1933–1941

N

1,500 miles

1,500 kilometers

750

750

0

0

© maps.com

Hawaii (U.S.)

PACIFIC

OCEAN

MARSHALL IS.

CAROLINE IS.

SOLOMON IS.

BONIN ISLANDS

GUAM

PALAU I.

NEW GUINEA

AUSTRALIA

SAKHALIN (KARAFUTO)

JAPAN

KOREA

Yellow Sea

East China Sea

FORMOSA

PHILIPPINES (U.S.)

Leyte Gulf

DUTCH EAST INDIES

CELEBES

MANCHUKUO (MANCHURIA) (1931–1932)

INNER MONGOLIA (1936)

OCCUPIED CHINA (1937–1938)

Hong Kong (Brit.)

MACAO

South China Sea

BORNEO

BRUNEI

SARAWAK

JAVA

SUMATRA

MONGOLIA

CHINA

FRENCH INDOCHINA (1941)

THAILAND (SIAM) (1941)

MALAYA (Brit.)

U.S.S.R.

BURMA

INDIA

WORLD WAR II, EUROPEAN THEATER, 1940–1945

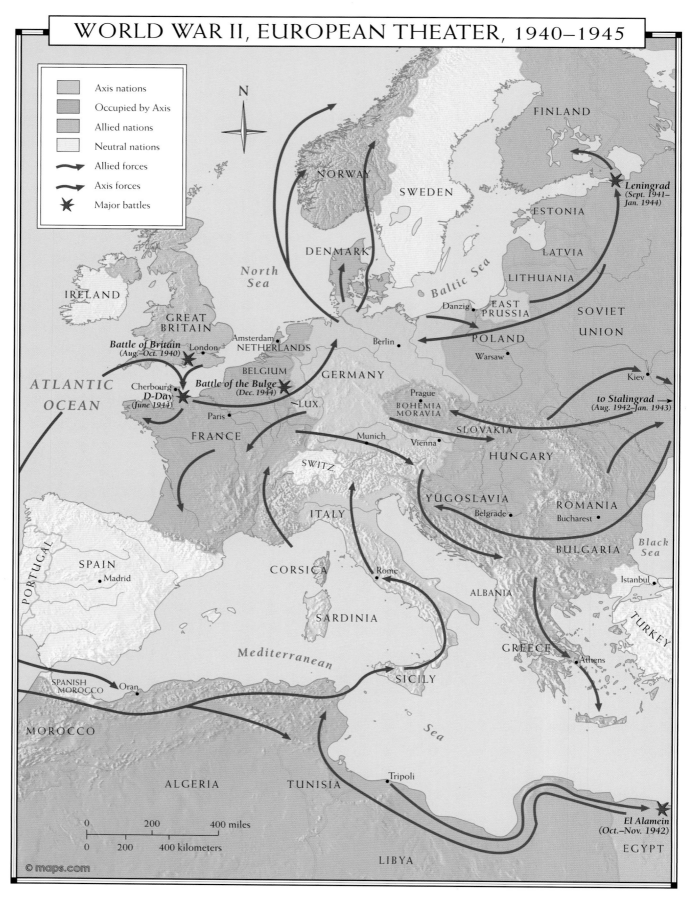

Legend:
- Axis nations
- Occupied by Axis
- Allied nations
- Neutral nations
- Allied forces
- Axis forces
- ✳ Major battles

N

FINLAND

SWEDEN

ESTONIA

LATVIA

LITHUANIA

✳ Leningrad
(Sept. 1941–Jan. 1944)

SOVIET UNION

NORWAY

DENMARK

North Sea

Baltic Sea

Danzig

EAST PRUSSIA

POLAND

Warsaw

to Stalingrad
(Aug. 1942–Jan. 1943)

Kiev

IRELAND

GREAT BRITAIN

Battle of Britain
(Aug.–Oct. 1940)

London

Amsterdam
NETHERLANDS

Berlin

ATLANTIC OCEAN

Cherbourg
D-Day
(June 1944)

BELGIUM

Battle of the Bulge
(Dec. 1944) ✳

LUX.

GERMANY

Prague
BOHEMIA
MORAVIA

Munich

Vienna

SLOVAKIA

HUNGARY

Paris

FRANCE

SWITZ.

ROMANIA

Bucharest

YUGOSLAVIA

Belgrade

PORTUGAL

SPAIN

Madrid

CORSICA

ITALY

Rome

SARDINIA

Mediterranean

ALBANIA

BULGARIA

Black Sea

Istanbul

TURKEY

GREECE

Athens

SPANISH MOROCCO

Oran

SICILY

Sea

MOROCCO

ALGERIA

TUNISIA

Tripoli

El Alamein
(Oct.–Nov. 1942) ✳

LIBYA

EGYPT

0   200   400 miles

0   200   400 kilometers

© maps.com

WORLD WAR II IN THE PACIFIC, 1941–1945

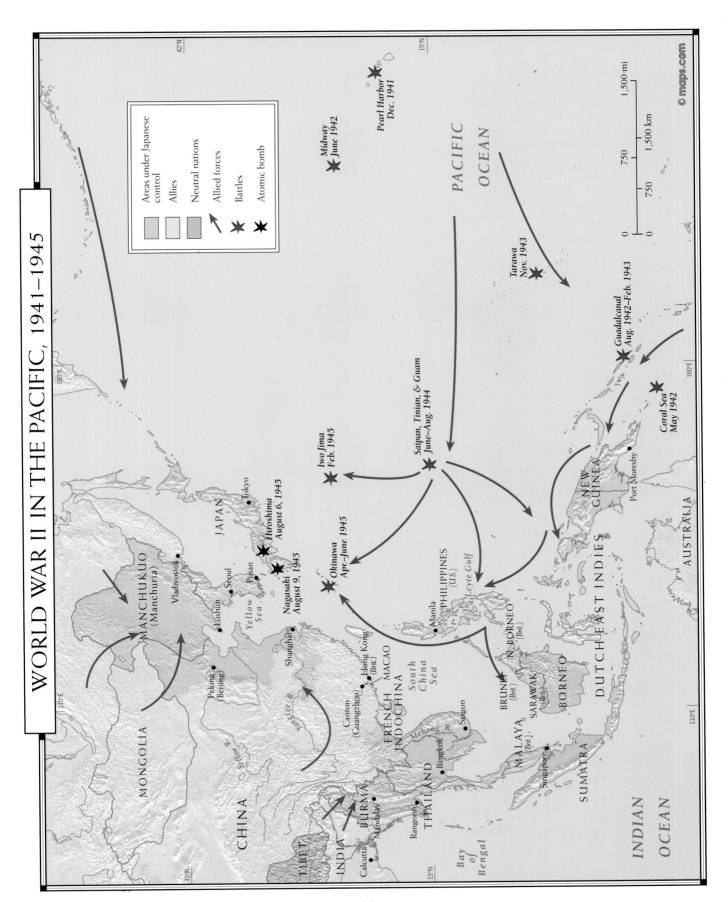

Areas under Japanese control
Allies
Neutral nations
Allied forces
Battles
Atomic bomb

Pearl Harbor
Dec. 1941

Midway
June 1942

PACIFIC OCEAN

Tarawa
Nov. 1943

Guadalcanal
Aug. 1942–Feb. 1943

Coral Sea
May 1942

Saipan, Tinian, & Guam
June–Aug. 1944

Iwo Jima
Feb. 1945

NEW GUINEA

Port Moresby

AUSTRALIA

Tokyo

JAPAN

Hiroshima
August 6, 1945

Vladivostok

MANCHUKUO
(Manchuria)

Fushun

Seoul

Pusan

Yellow Sea

Nagasaki
August 9, 1945

Okinawa
Apr–June 1945

Shanghai

PHILIPPINES
(U.S.)

Leyte Gulf

Manila

N. BORNEO
(Brit.)

MONGOLIA

Peking
(Beijing)

CHINA

Yangtze R.

Canton
(Guangzhou)

Hong Kong
(Brit.)

MACAO

FRENCH INDOCHINA

South China Sea

BRUNEI
(Brit.)

SARAWAK
(Brit.)

BORNEO

DUTCH EAST INDIES

Saigon

Mekong R.

MALAYA
(Brit.)

Singapore
(Brit.)

SUMATRA

Bangkok

THAILAND

Rangoon

BURMA

Mandalay

INDIA

Calcutta

TIBET

Bay of Bengal

INDIAN OCEAN

1,500 mi
1,500 km
750
750
0
0

© maps.com

INDEPENDENT STATES TO 1991

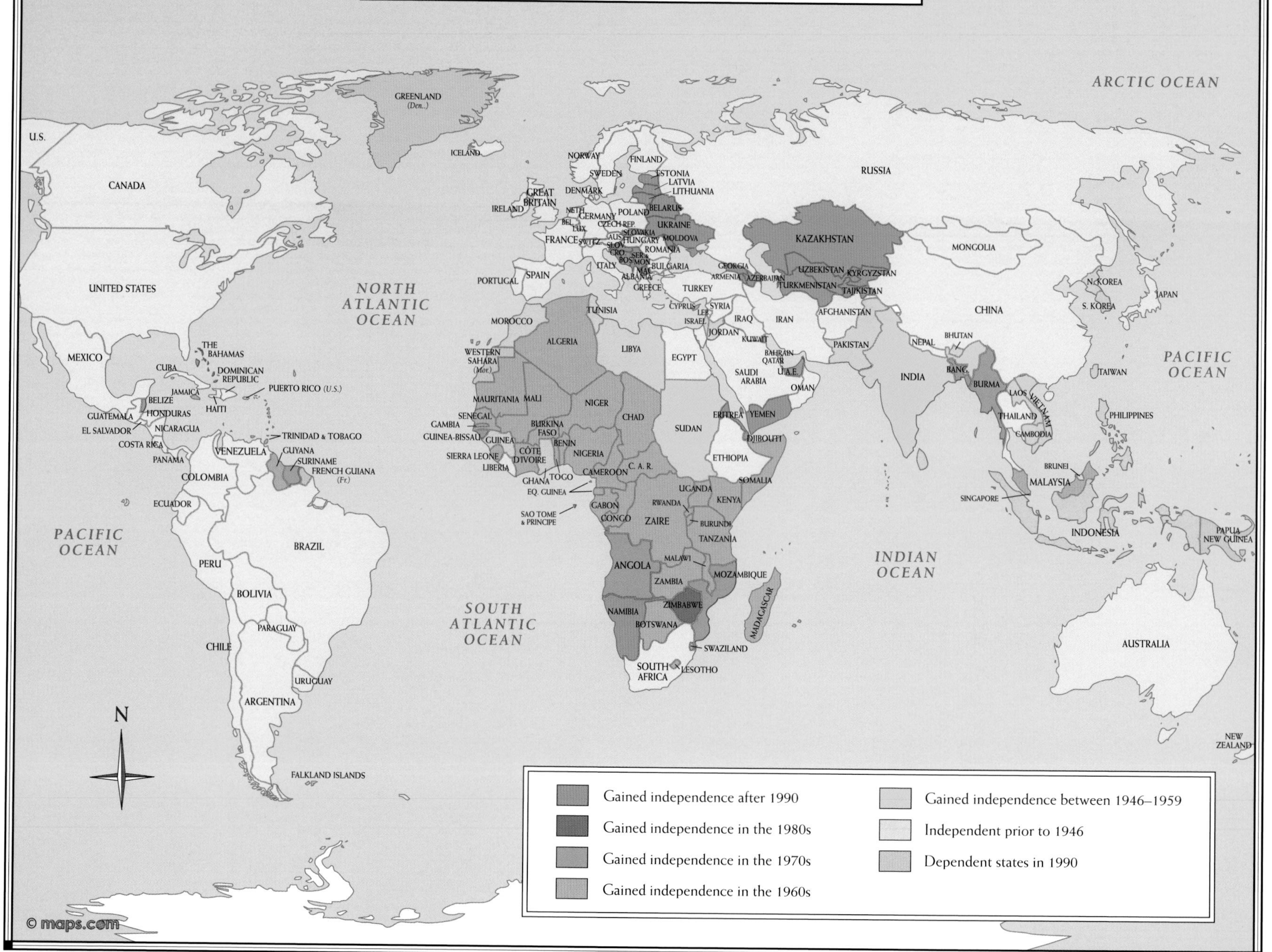

Legend:

- Gained independence between 1946–1959
- Independent prior to 1946
- Dependent states in 1990
- Gained independence after 1990
- Gained independence in the 1980s
- Gained independence in the 1970s
- Gained independence in the 1960s

Oceans:
ARCTIC OCEAN · PACIFIC OCEAN · INDIAN OCEAN · NORTH ATLANTIC OCEAN · SOUTH ATLANTIC OCEAN

Labels on map:

NEW ZEALAND, PAPUA NEW GUINEA, AUSTRALIA, INDONESIA, PHILIPPINES, TAIWAN, JAPAN, N. KOREA, S. KOREA, BRUNEI, MALAYSIA, SINGAPORE, VIETNAM, LAOS, CAMBODIA, THAILAND, BURMA, BANG. (Bangladesh), BHUTAN, NEPAL, CHINA, MONGOLIA, INDIA, PAKISTAN, AFGHANISTAN, RUSSIA, KAZAKHSTAN, UZBEKISTAN, KYRGYZSTAN, TAJIKISTAN, TURKMENISTAN, IRAN, OMAN, U.A.E., QATAR, BAHRAIN, SAUDI ARABIA, KUWAIT, IRAQ, YEMEN, DJIBOUTI, ERITREA, ETHIOPIA, SOMALIA, KENYA, TANZANIA, BURUNDI, RWANDA, UGANDA, ZAIRE, SUDAN, C.A.R., CHAD, CONGO, GABON, CAMEROON, NIGERIA, NIGER, EQ. GUINEA, SAO TOME & PRINCIPE, GHANA, TOGO, BENIN, BURKINA FASO, COTE D'IVOIRE, LIBERIA, SIERRA LEONE, GUINEA, GUINEA-BISSAU, GAMBIA, SENEGAL, MAURITANIA, MALI, WESTERN SAHARA (Mor.), MOROCCO, ALGERIA, TUNISIA, LIBYA, EGYPT, ANGOLA, ZAMBIA, MALAWI, ZIMBABWE, MOZAMBIQUE, NAMIBIA, BOTSWANA, SOUTH AFRICA, SWAZILAND, LESOTHO, MADAGASCAR, TURKEY, CYPRUS, LEB. (Lebanon), SYRIA, ISRAEL, JORDAN, GEORGIA, ARMENIA, AZERBAIJAN, GREECE, ALBANIA, BULGARIA, ROMANIA, MOLDOVA, UKRAINE, BELARUS, POLAND, CZECHO., SLOVAKIA, HUNGARY, YUGO., CRO., SLO., AUS. (Austria), ITALY, SWITZ., FRANCE, GERMANY, NETH. (Netherlands), BEL. (Belgium), LUX., DENMARK, LATVIA, LITHUANIA, ESTONIA, FINLAND, SWEDEN, NORWAY, GREAT BRITAIN, IRELAND, SPAIN, PORTUGAL, ICELAND, GREENLAND (Dm.), CANADA, UNITED STATES, U.S., MEXICO, GUATEMALA, BELIZE, EL SALVADOR, HONDURAS, NICARAGUA, COSTA RICA, PANAMA, CUBA, JAMAICA, THE BAHAMAS, HAITI, DOMINICAN REPUBLIC, PUERTO RICO (U.S.), TRINIDAD & TOBAGO, VENEZUELA, COLOMBIA, ECUADOR, PERU, GUYANA, SURINAME, FRENCH GUIANA (Fr.), BRAZIL, BOLIVIA, PARAGUAY, URUGUAY, ARGENTINA, CHILE, FALKLAND ISLANDS

N (compass)

© maps.com

COLD WAR EUROPE, 1946–1990

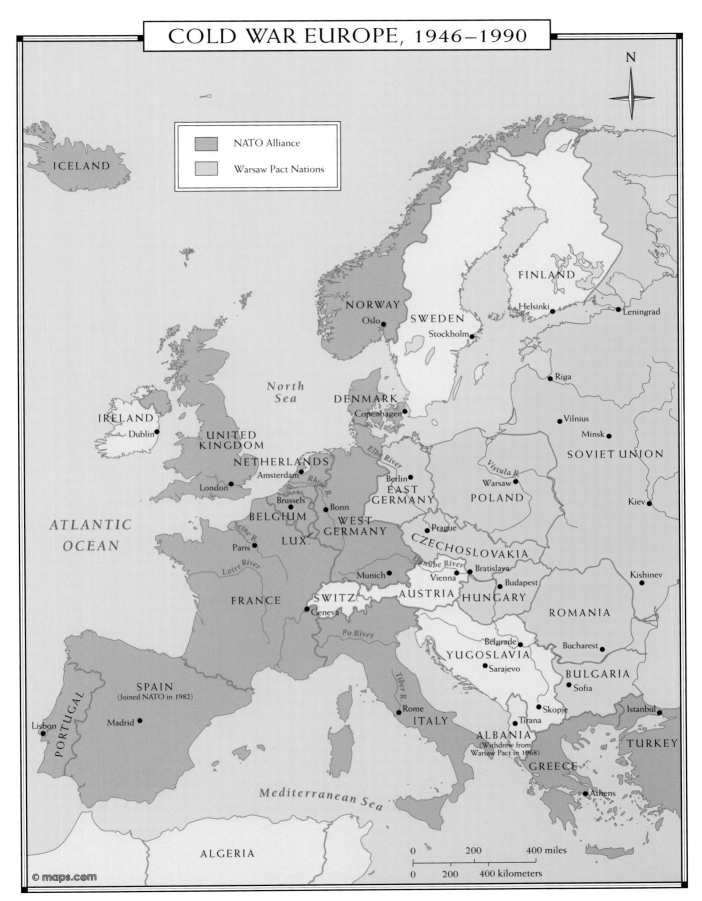

N

■	NATO Alliance
■	Warsaw Pact Nations

ICELAND

FINLAND
Helsinki •
• Leningrad

NORWAY
Oslo •

SWEDEN
Stockholm •

Riga •

North
Sea

DENMARK
Copenhagen •

Vilnius •

Minsk •

SOVIET UNION

IRELAND
Dublin •

UNITED
KINGDOM

NETHERLANDS
Amsterdam •

Berlin •

Warsaw •

Kiev •

London •

Rhine R.

EAST
GERMANY

Vistula R.

POLAND

Brussels •

Bonn •

BELGIUM

WEST
GERMANY

Prague •

ATLANTIC
OCEAN

Seine R.

LUX.

CZECHOSLOVAKIA

Kishinev •

Paris •

Munich •

Danube River

Vienna •

Bratislava •

Loire River

SWITZ.
Geneva •

AUSTRIA

Budapest •

HUNGARY

ROMANIA

FRANCE

Po River

Belgrade •

Bucharest •

SPAIN
(Joined NATO in 1982)

YUGOSLAVIA

Sarajevo •

BULGARIA
Sofia •

PORTUGAL

Madrid •

Tiber R.

Rome •

ITALY

Skopje •

Tirana •

ALBANIA
(Withdrew from
Warsaw Pact in 1968)

Istanbul •

TURKEY

Lisbon •

GREECE

Mediterranean Sea

Athens •

ALGERIA

0		200		400 miles
0	200		400 kilometers	

© maps.com

– 43 –

THE VIETNAM WAR, 1964–1975

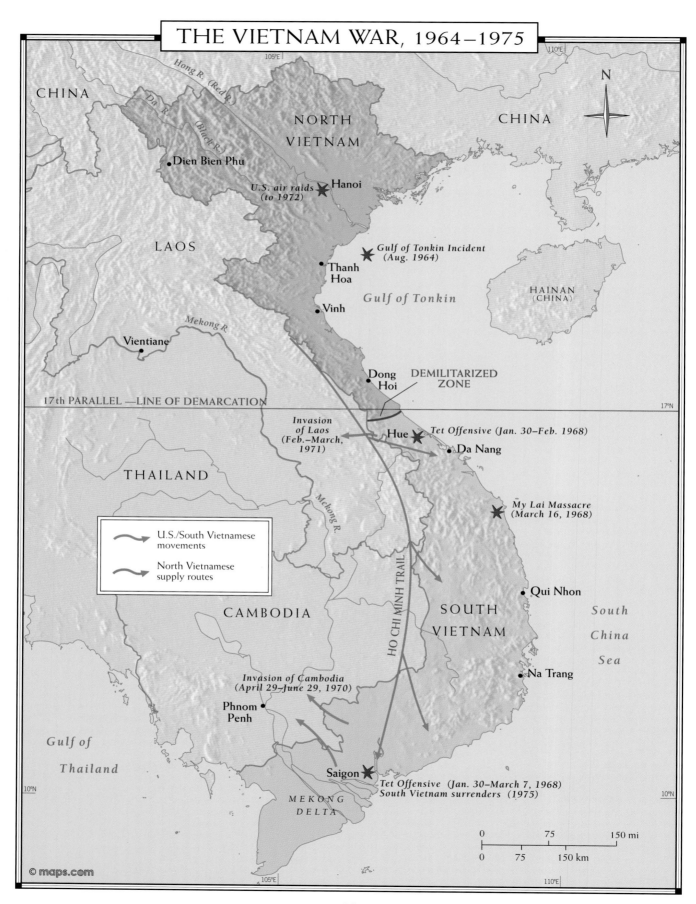

CHINA

Hong R. (Red R.)

Da R.

Black R.

NORTH VIETNAM

CHINA

N

• Dien Bien Phu

U.S. air raids (to 1972) ✴ Hanoi

LAOS

Gulf of Tonkin Incident (Aug. 1964) ✴

• Thanh Hoa

Gulf of Tonkin

HAINAN (CHINA)

• Vinh

Mekong R.

Vientiane •

Dong Hoi • DEMILITARIZED ZONE

17th PARALLEL — LINE OF DEMARCATION

17°N

Invasion of Laos (Feb.–March, 1971) Hue • ✴ *Tet Offensive (Jan. 30–Feb. 1968)*

• Da Nang

THAILAND

Mekong R.

My Lai Massacre (March 16, 1968) ✴

| | U.S./South Vietnamese movements |
| ⟶ | North Vietnamese supply routes |

CAMBODIA

HO CHI MINH TRAIL

SOUTH VIETNAM

• Qui Nhon

South China Sea

• Na Trang

Invasion of Cambodia (April 29–June 29, 1970)

Phnom Penh •

Gulf of Thailand

Saigon • ✴

Tet Offensive (Jan. 30–March 7, 1968)
South Vietnam surrenders (1975)

10°N

MEKONG DELTA

| 0 | | 75 | | 150 mi |
| 0 | | 75 | 150 km | |

10°N

© maps.com

STATES OF THE WORLD, 2003

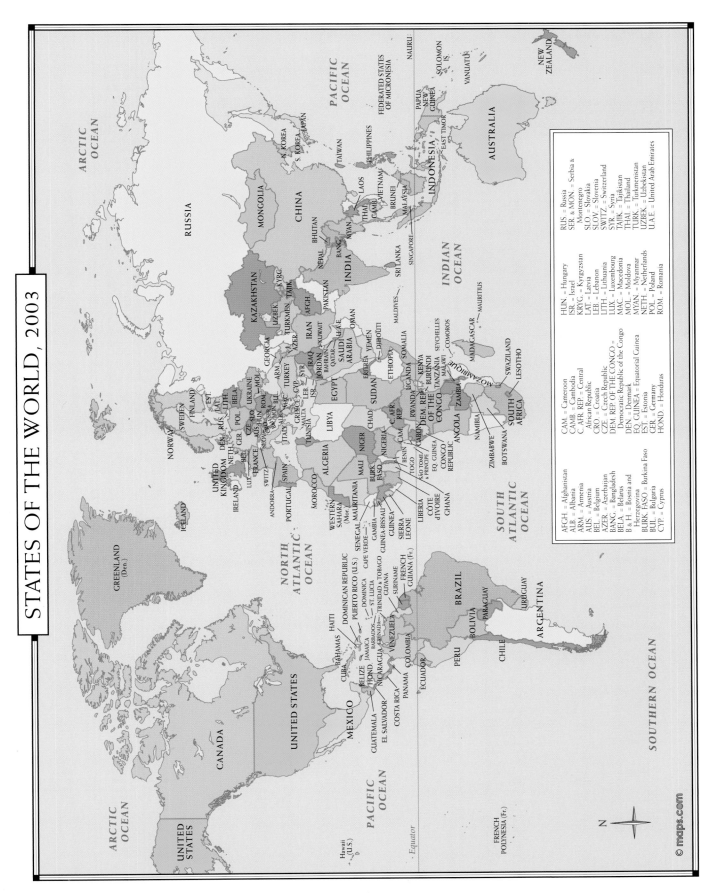

© maps.com

INDEX